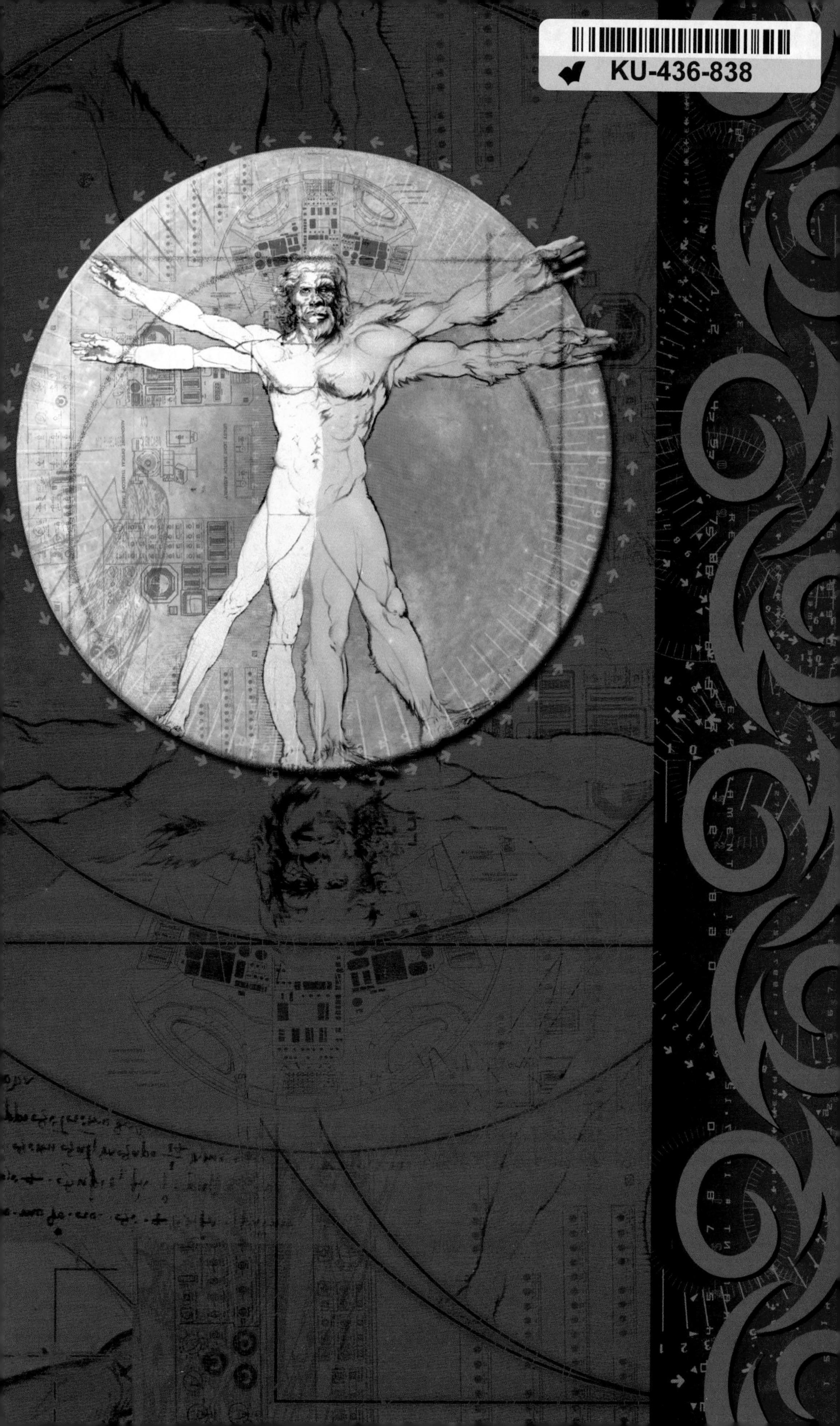

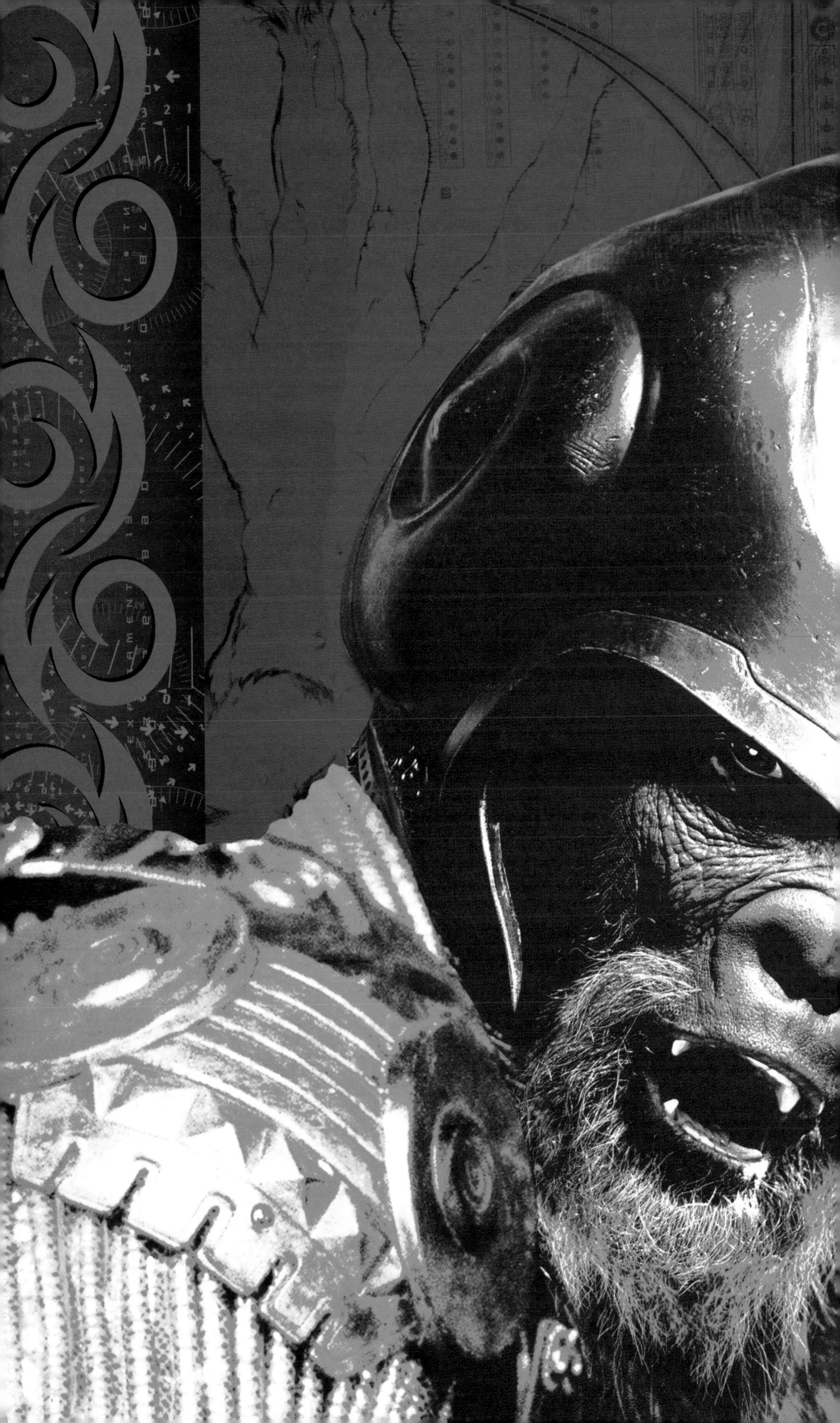

PLANET OF THE APES

ADAPTED FOR COMICS BY:

WRITER

SCOTT ALLIE

PENCILS

DAVIDÉ FABBRI

INKS

CHRISTIAN DALLA VECCHIA
WITH **CHRISTOPHER IVY**

COLORS

DAVE STEWART

LETTERING

PAT BROSSEAU

Titan
BOOKS

USAF OBERON
CREW LOG
VOICE ACTIVATED:
21:46:23 02-06-2029

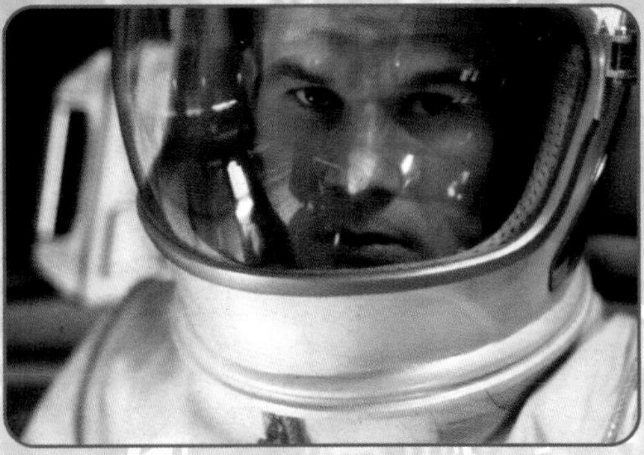

MAJOR LEO DAVIDSON
FLIGHT WING COMMANDER

In the A.M., we're doing a flight sim with Pericles — my protégé. Trying to throw him a curveball. Grace, if you're reading this — busted! —you're missing the point with our little chimp. Control groups and repetitious test conditions are fine if you're trying to understand chemical reactions, subatomic reactions, but adaptability and thinking on your feet make the difference between a pilot and just another trained monkey.

You said there's only a two percent difference between man and ape — with Pericles and these other state-of-the-art monkeys, less than one percent. Anyway, I'll leave that stuff to your log. Pericles is doing better in his dry runs, getting his pod back to the *Oberon* with the same dexterity as a commercial flier back home. He's no soldier yet. Still, I envy the hairy little guy. He's flying once or twice a day now, doing great, and it's starting to look like he has a lady friend. Kind of "the girl next door," except next door's another three-by-three cage. Can't say I have it much better on the *Oberon*. Haven't been behind real controls in over three weeks. Maybe in my dreams.

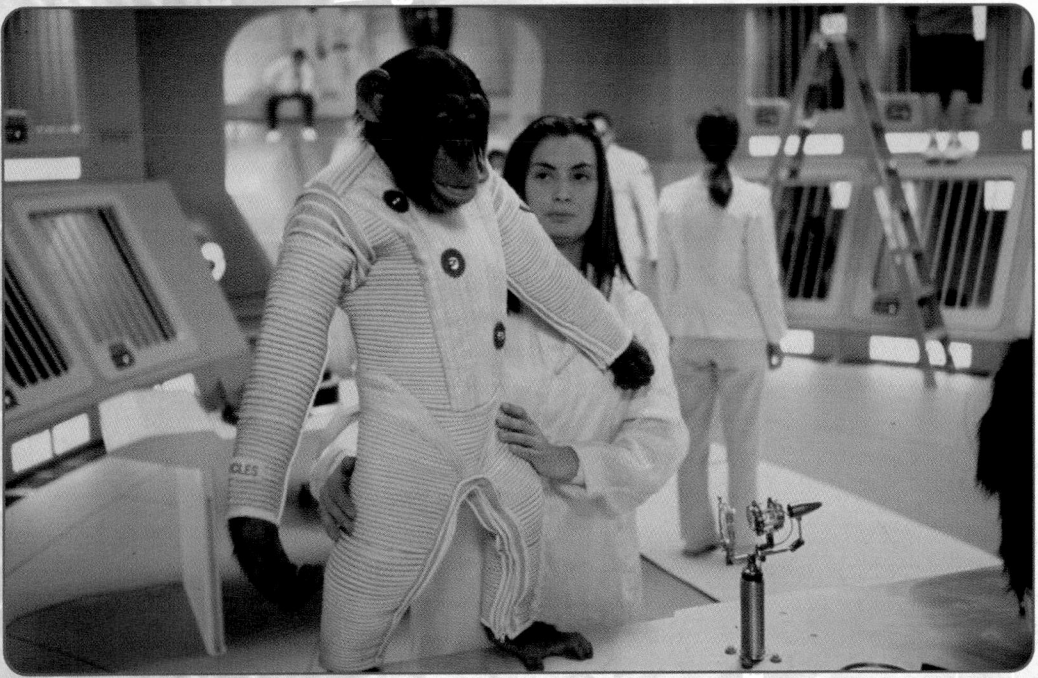

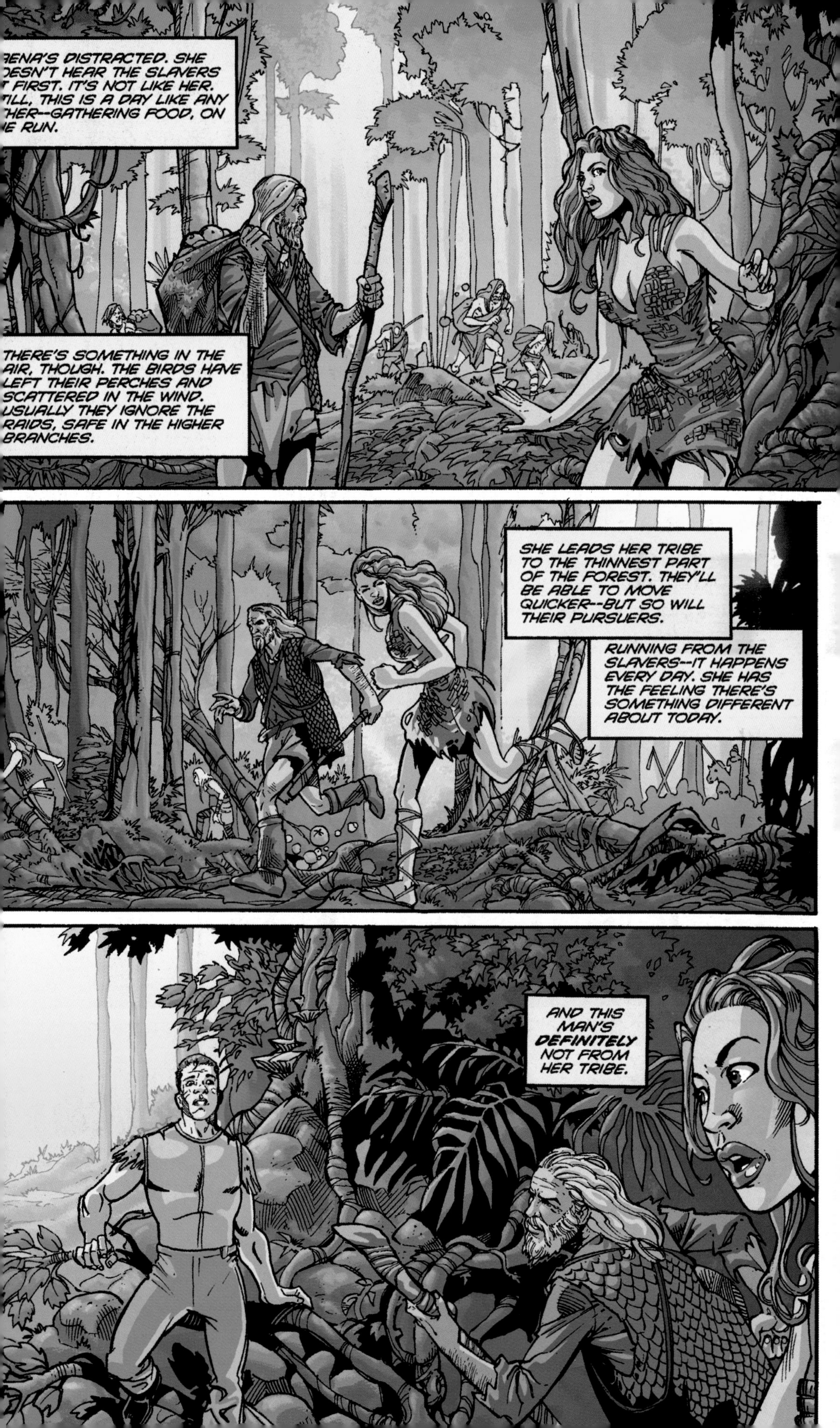
ƎENA'S DISTRACTED. SHE
OESN'T HEAR THE SLAVERS
FIRST. IT'S NOT LIKE HER.
TILL, THIS IS A DAY LIKE ANY
THER--GATHERING FOOD, ON
E RUN.
THERE'S SOMETHING IN THE AIR, THOUGH. THE BIRDS HAVE LEFT THEIR PERCHES AND SCATTERED IN THE WIND. USUALLY THEY IGNORE THE RAIDS, SAFE IN THE HIGHER BRANCHES.
SHE LEADS HER TRIBE TO THE THINNEST PART OF THE FOREST. THEY'LL BE ABLE TO MOVE QUICKER--BUT SO WILL THEIR PURSUERS.
RUNNING FROM THE SLAVERS--IT HAPPENS EVERY DAY. SHE HAS THE FEELING THERE'S SOMETHING DIFFERENT ABOUT TODAY.
AND THIS MAN'S **DEFINITELY** NOT FROM HER TRIBE.

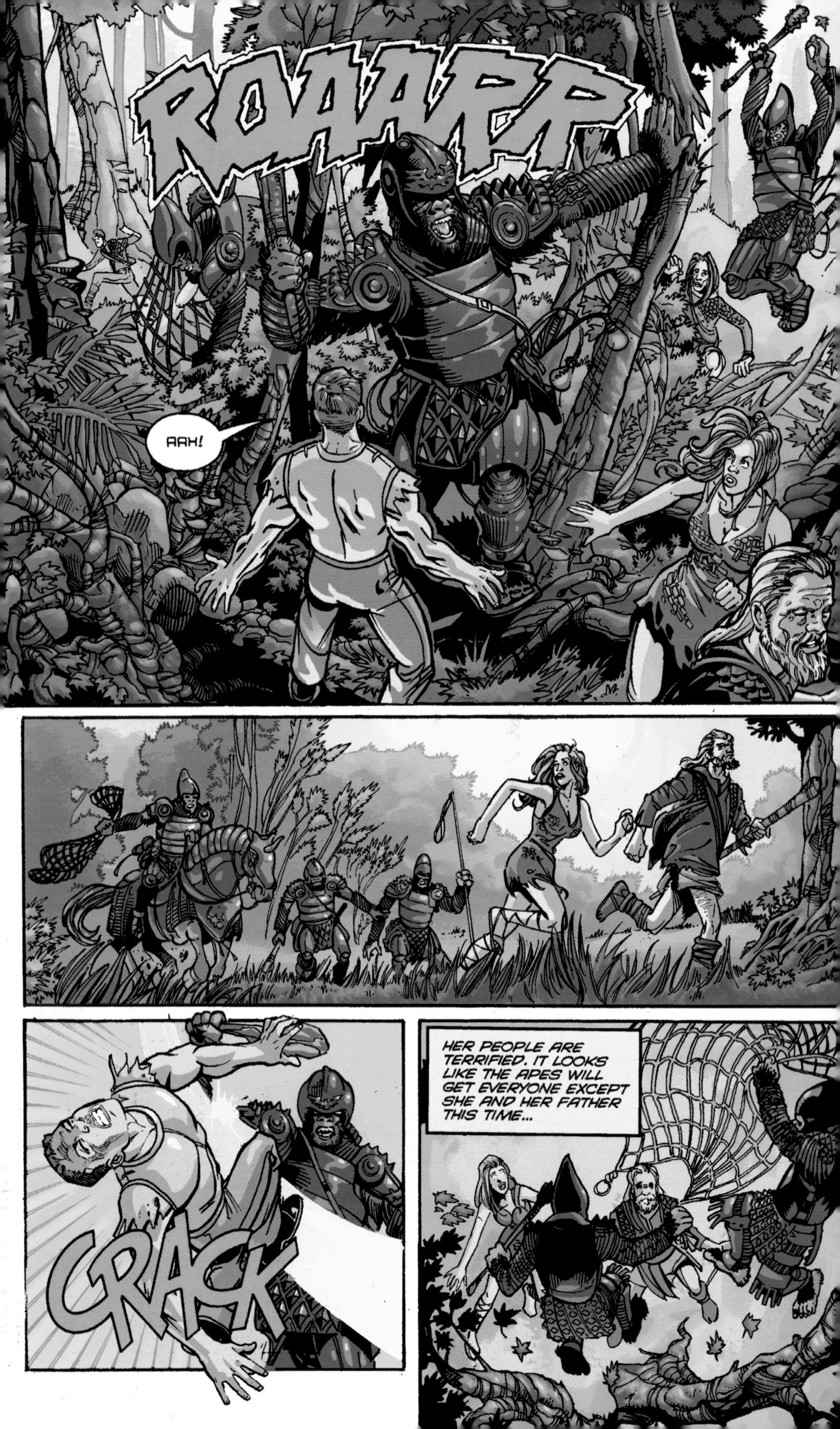
ROAAPP
AAH!
CRACK
HER PEOPLE ARE TERRIFIED. IT LOOKS LIKE THE APES WILL GET EVERYONE EXCEPT SHE AND HER FATHER THIS TIME...

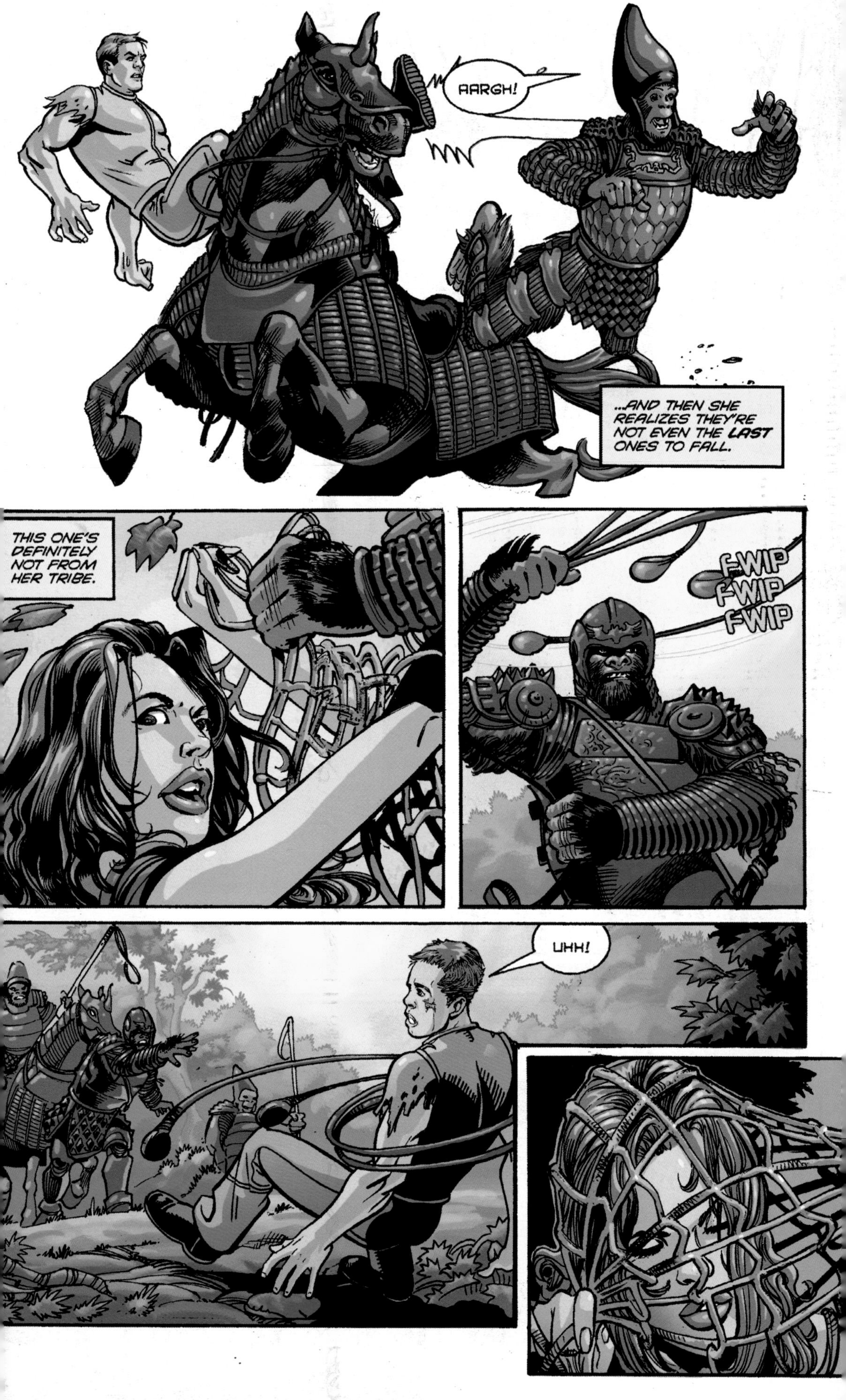
AARGH!
...AND THEN SHE REALIZES THEY'RE NOT EVEN THE LAST ONES TO FALL.
THIS ONE'S DEFINITELY NOT FROM HER TRIBE.
FWIP FWIP FWIP
UHH!

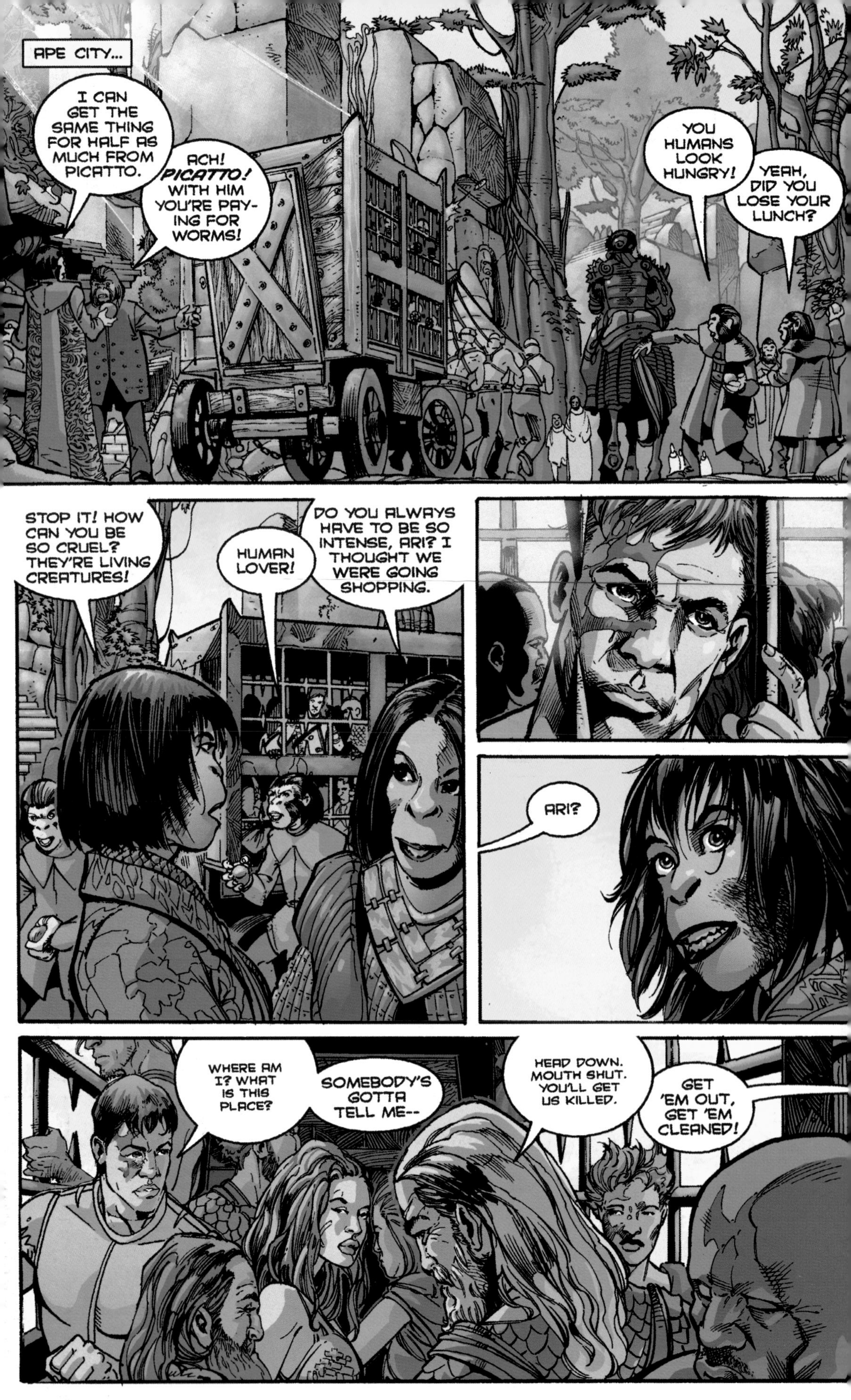
APE CITY...
I CAN GET THE SAME THING FOR HALF AS MUCH FROM PICATTO.
ACH! PICATTO! WITH HIM YOU'RE PAYING FOR WORMS!
YOU HUMANS LOOK HUNGRY!
YEAH, DID YOU LOSE YOUR LUNCH?
STOP IT! HOW CAN YOU BE SO CRUEL? THEY'RE LIVING CREATURES!
HUMAN LOVER!
DO YOU ALWAYS HAVE TO BE SO INTENSE, ARI? I THOUGHT WE WERE GOING SHOPPING.
ARI?
WHERE AM I? WHAT IS THIS PLACE?
SOMEBODY'S GOTTA TELL ME--
HEAD DOWN. MOUTH SHUT. YOU'LL GET US KILLED.
GET 'EM OUT, GET 'EM CLEANED!

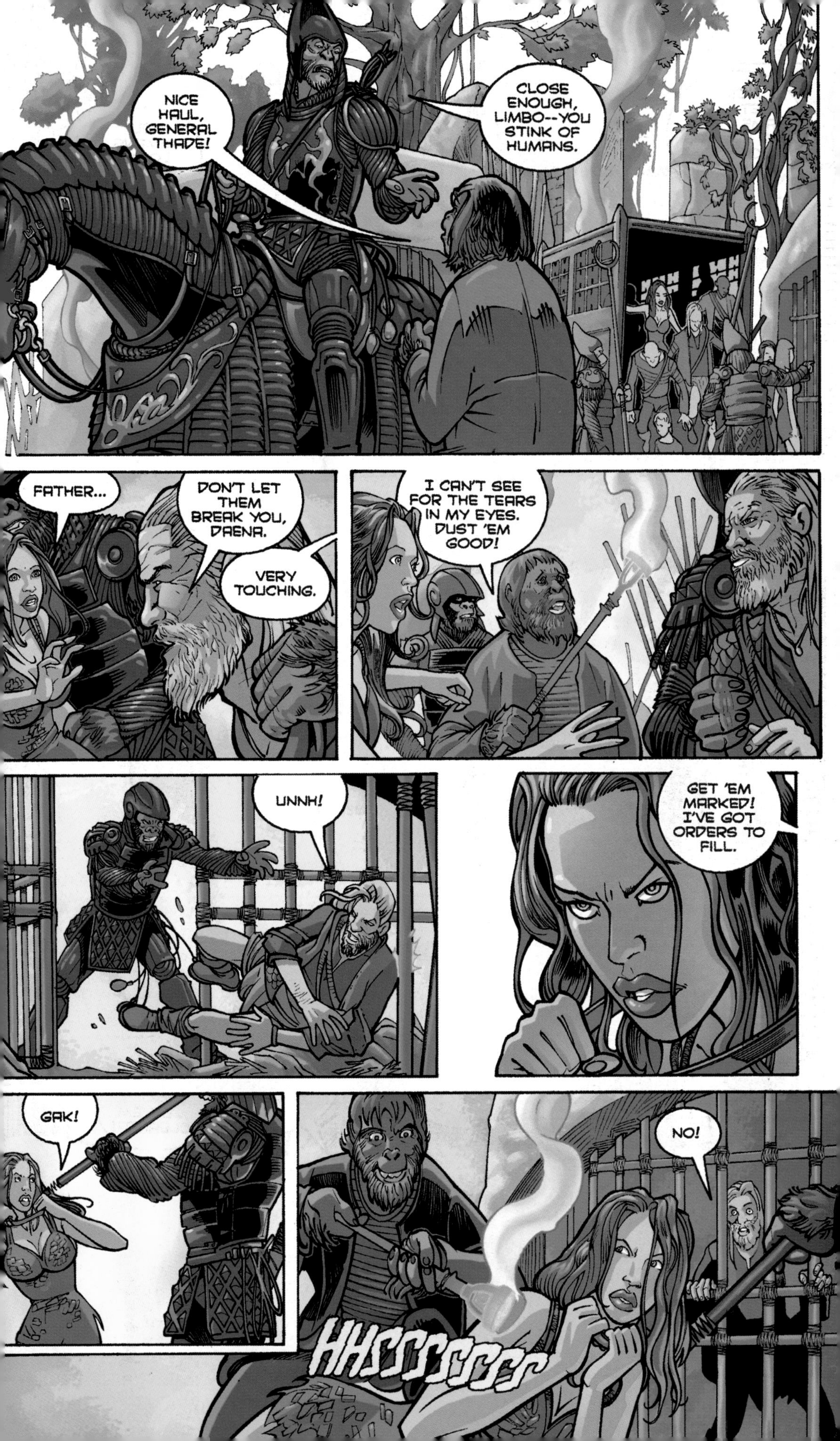

NICE HAUL, GENERAL THADE!
CLOSE ENOUGH, LIMBO--YOU STINK OF HUMANS.
FATHER...
DON'T LET THEM BREAK YOU, DAENA.
VERY TOUCHING.
I CAN'T SEE FOR THE TEARS IN MY EYES. DUST 'EM GOOD!
UNNH!
GET 'EM MARKED! I'VE GOT ORDERS TO FILL.
GAK!
NO!
HHSSSSSSS

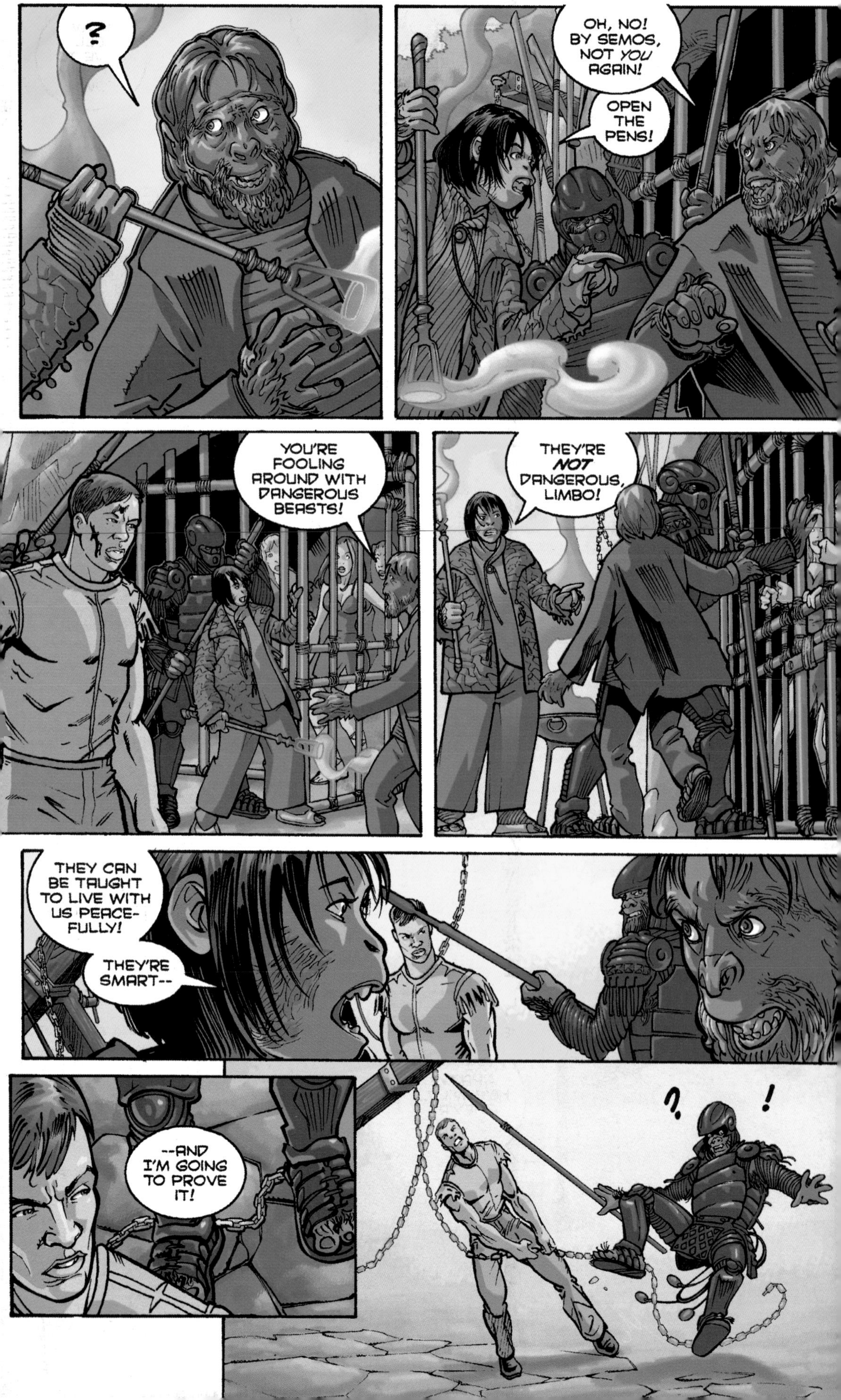
?
OH, NO! BY SEMOS, NOT YOU AGAIN!
OPEN THE PENS!
YOU'RE FOOLING AROUND WITH DANGEROUS BEASTS!
THEY'RE NOT DANGEROUS, LIMBO!
THEY CAN BE TAUGHT TO LIVE WITH US PEACE-FULLY!
THEY'RE SMART--
--AND I'M GOING TO PROVE IT!
?
!

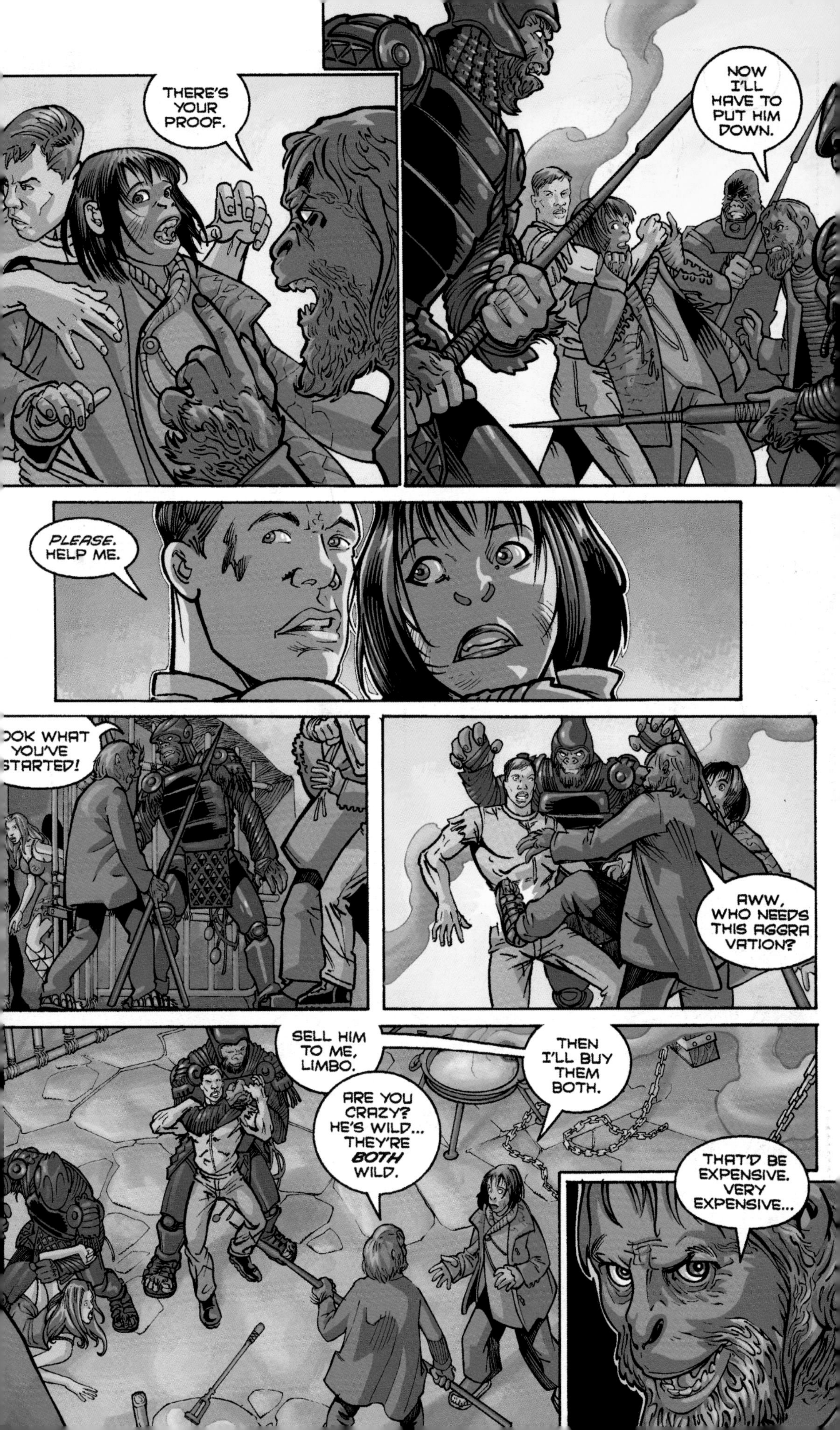
THERE'S YOUR PROOF.
NOW I'LL HAVE TO PUT HIM DOWN.
PLEASE. HELP ME.
OOK WHAT YOU'VE STARTED!
AWW, WHO NEEDS THIS AGGRA VATION?
SELL HIM TO ME, LIMBO.
ARE YOU CRAZY? HE'S WILD... THEY'RE BOTH WILD.
THEN I'LL BUY THEM BOTH.
THAT'D BE EXPENSIVE. VERY EXPENSIVE...

HOW DID THESE MONKEYS GET THIS WAY?!

WHAT OTHER WAY WOULD THEY BE?

BEGGING FOR A TREAT.

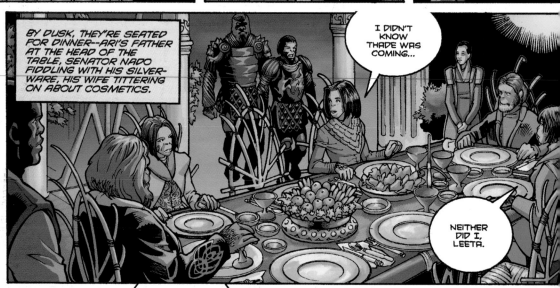

BY DUSK, THEY'RE SEATED FOR DINNER--ARI'S FATHER AT THE HEAD OF THE TABLE, SENATOR NADO FIDDLING WITH HIS SILVER-WARE, HIS WIFE TITTERING ON ABOUT COSMETICS.

I DIDN'T KNOW THADE WAS COMING...

NEITHER DID I, LEETA.

WE THANK SEMOS, HOLY FATHER OF ALL APES, AND PRAY FOR THE DAY WHEN HE WILL RETURN.

AMEN.

WHAT IS THIS BEAST DOING IN YOUR HOUSE?!

I BOUGHT HIM.

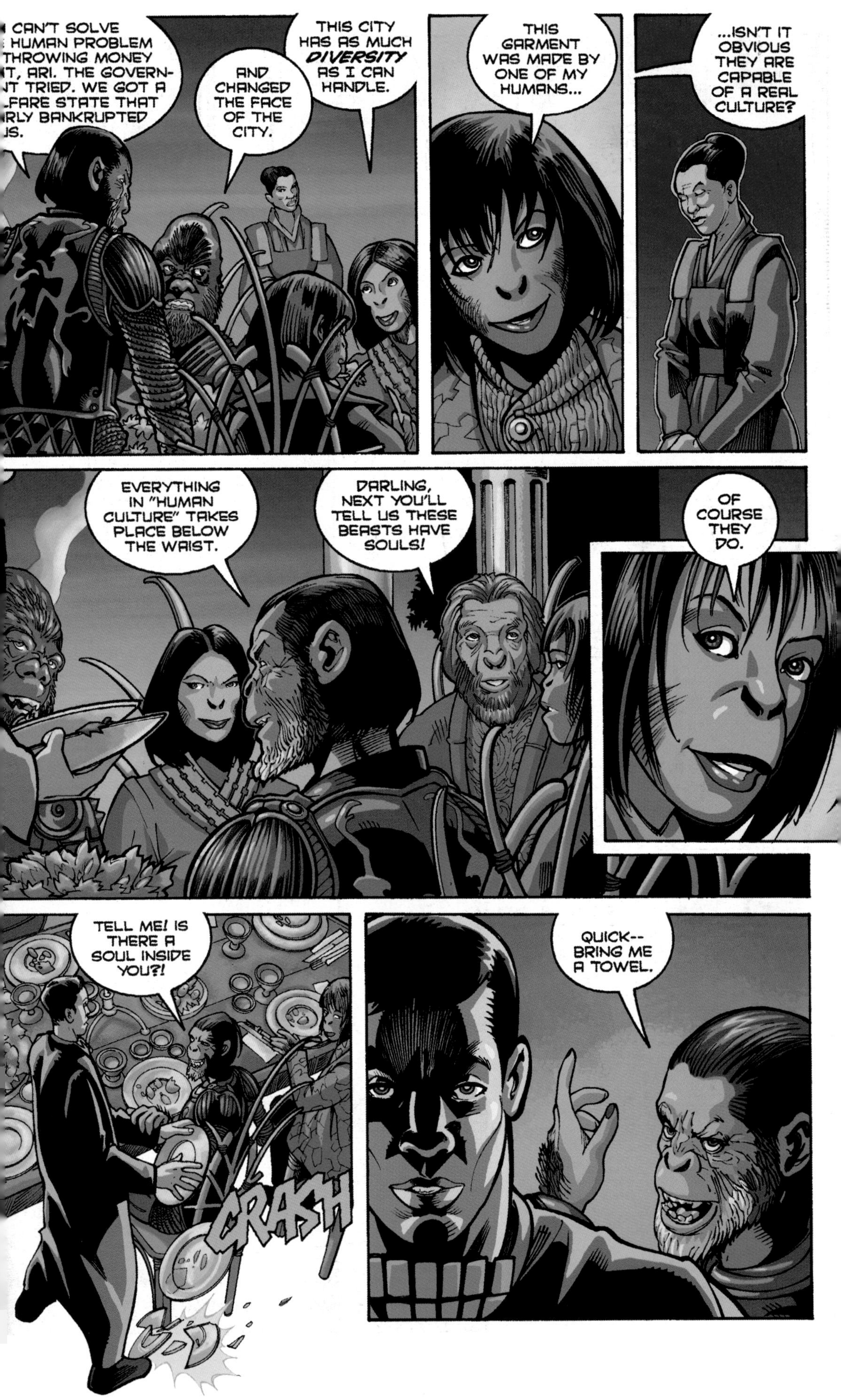
CAN'T SOLVE HUMAN PROBLEM THROWING MONEY T, ARI. THE GOVERN- NT TRIED. WE GOT A LFARE STATE THAT RLY BANKRUPTED US.
AND CHANGED THE FACE OF THE CITY.
THIS CITY HAS AS MUCH DIVERSITY AS I CAN HANDLE.
THIS GARMENT WAS MADE BY ONE OF MY HUMANS...
...ISN'T IT OBVIOUS THEY ARE CAPABLE OF A REAL CULTURE?
EVERYTHING IN "HUMAN CULTURE" TAKES PLACE BELOW THE WAIST.
DARLING, NEXT YOU'LL TELL US THESE BEASTS HAVE SOULS!
OF COURSE THEY DO.
TELL ME! IS THERE A SOUL INSIDE YOU?!
CRASH
QUICK-- BRING ME A TOWEL.

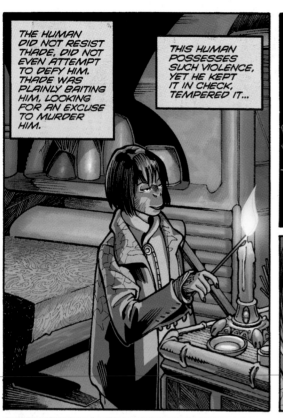

THE HUMAN DID NOT RESIST THADE, DID NOT EVEN ATTEMPT TO DEFY HIM. THADE WAS PLAINLY BAITING HIM, LOOKING FOR AN EXCUSE TO MURDER HIM.

THIS HUMAN POSSESSES SUCH VIOLENCE, YET HE KEPT IT IN CHECK, TEMPERED IT...

THADE COMES TO ARI IN HER ROOM AND TRIES TO ROMANCE HER, TO REKINDLE WHAT THEY ONCE SHARED.

YOU UNDER-ESTIMATE HOW HARD THIS IS FOR ME. GENTLE WORDS DO NOT COME EASY TO A SOLDIER.

THERE IS NOTHING GENTLE IN THADE.

BEFORE HE LEAVES, HIS ATTEMPT AT SEDUCTION HAS DEVOLVED INTO THREATS.

LEETA WILL HAVE GONE HOME BY NOW, LEAVING ARI ALONE TO CONSIDER WHAT HAPPENED TONIGHT. WHAT LINGERS FOREMOST IN HER MIND...

...IS THIS STRANGE HUMAN, WHO HAS SUCH AWARENESS ...SUCH CLEAR IN-TELLIGENCE.

CLICK

BUT OUR MISTRESS HAS BEEN SO KIND TO US...

SHE'S YOUR ENEMY.

CAN YOU FIND YOUR WAY BACK TO WHERE WE WERE CAPTURED?

FIRST WE GET MY FATHER.

TOO DANGEROUS.

THEN FIND YOUR OWN WAY BACK.

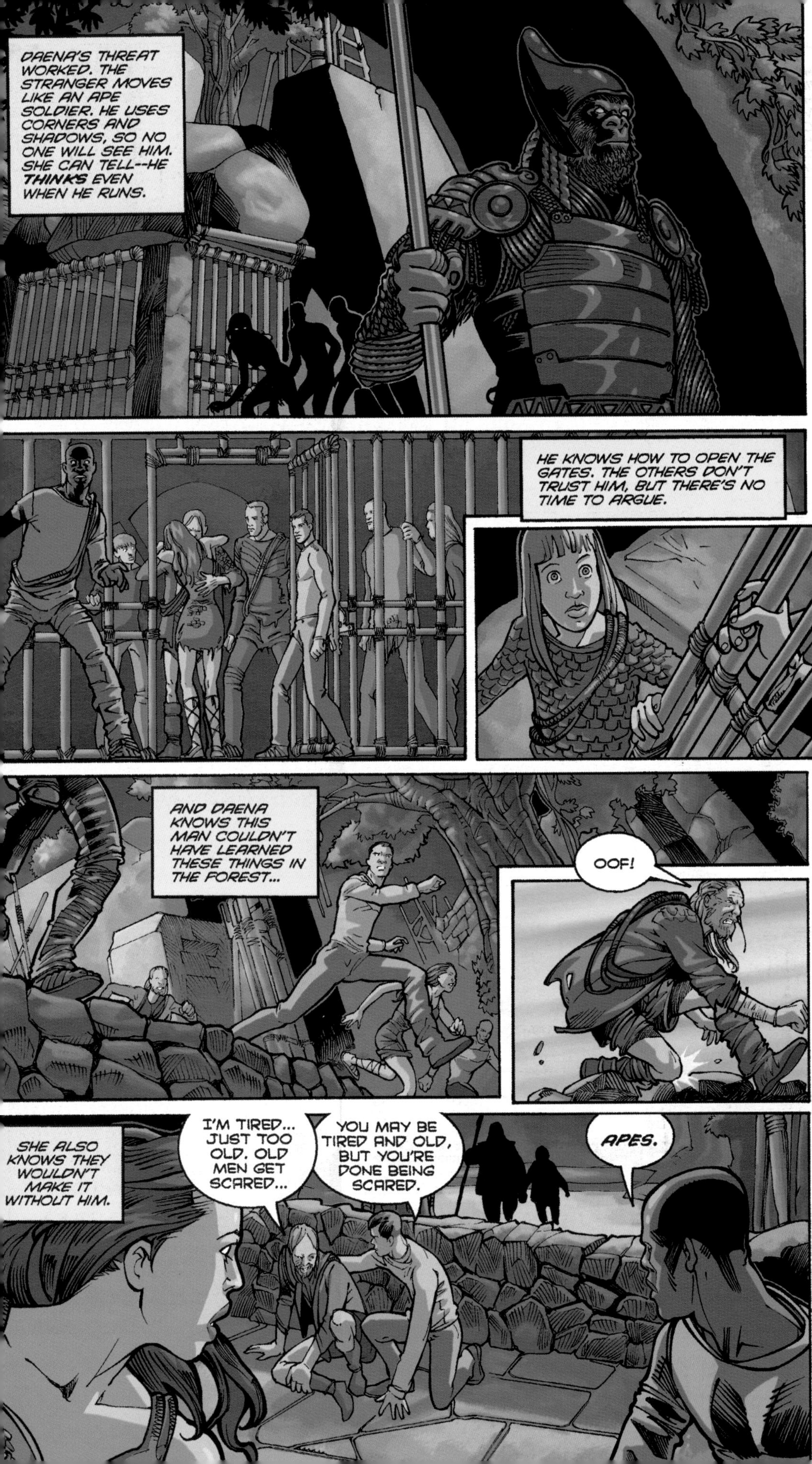
DAENA'S THREAT WORKED. THE STRANGER MOVES LIKE AN APE SOLDIER. HE USES CORNERS AND SHADOWS, SO NO ONE WILL SEE HIM. SHE CAN TELL--HE **THINKS** EVEN WHEN HE RUNS.
HE KNOWS HOW TO OPEN THE GATES. THE OTHERS DON'T TRUST HIM, BUT THERE'S NO TIME TO ARGUE.
AND DAENA KNOWS THIS MAN COULDN'T HAVE LEARNED THESE THINGS IN THE FOREST...
OOF!
SHE ALSO KNOWS THEY WOULDN'T MAKE IT WITHOUT HIM.
I'M TIRED... JUST TOO OLD. OLD MEN GET SCARED...
YOU MAY BE TIRED AND OLD, BUT YOU'RE DONE BEING SCARED.
APES.

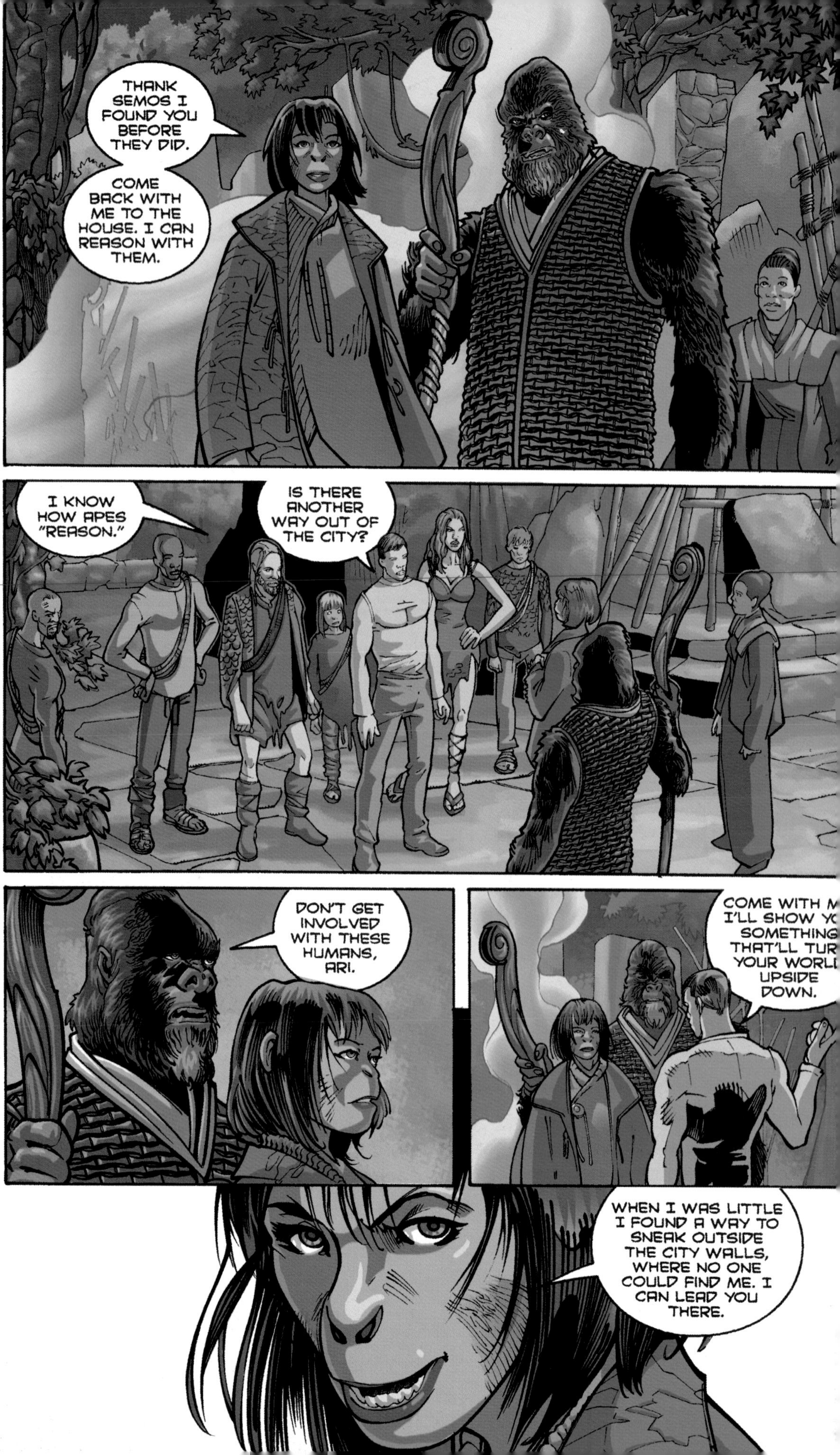
THANK SEMOS I FOUND YOU BEFORE THEY DID.
COME BACK WITH ME TO THE HOUSE. I CAN REASON WITH THEM.
I KNOW HOW APES "REASON."
IS THERE ANOTHER WAY OUT OF THE CITY?
DON'T GET INVOLVED WITH THESE HUMANS, ARI.
COME WITH M
I'LL SHOW YO
SOMETHING
THAT'LL TUR
YOUR WORL
UPSIDE DOWN.
WHEN I WAS LITTLE I FOUND A WAY TO SNEAK OUTSIDE THE CITY WALLS, WHERE NO ONE COULD FIND ME. I CAN LEAD YOU THERE.

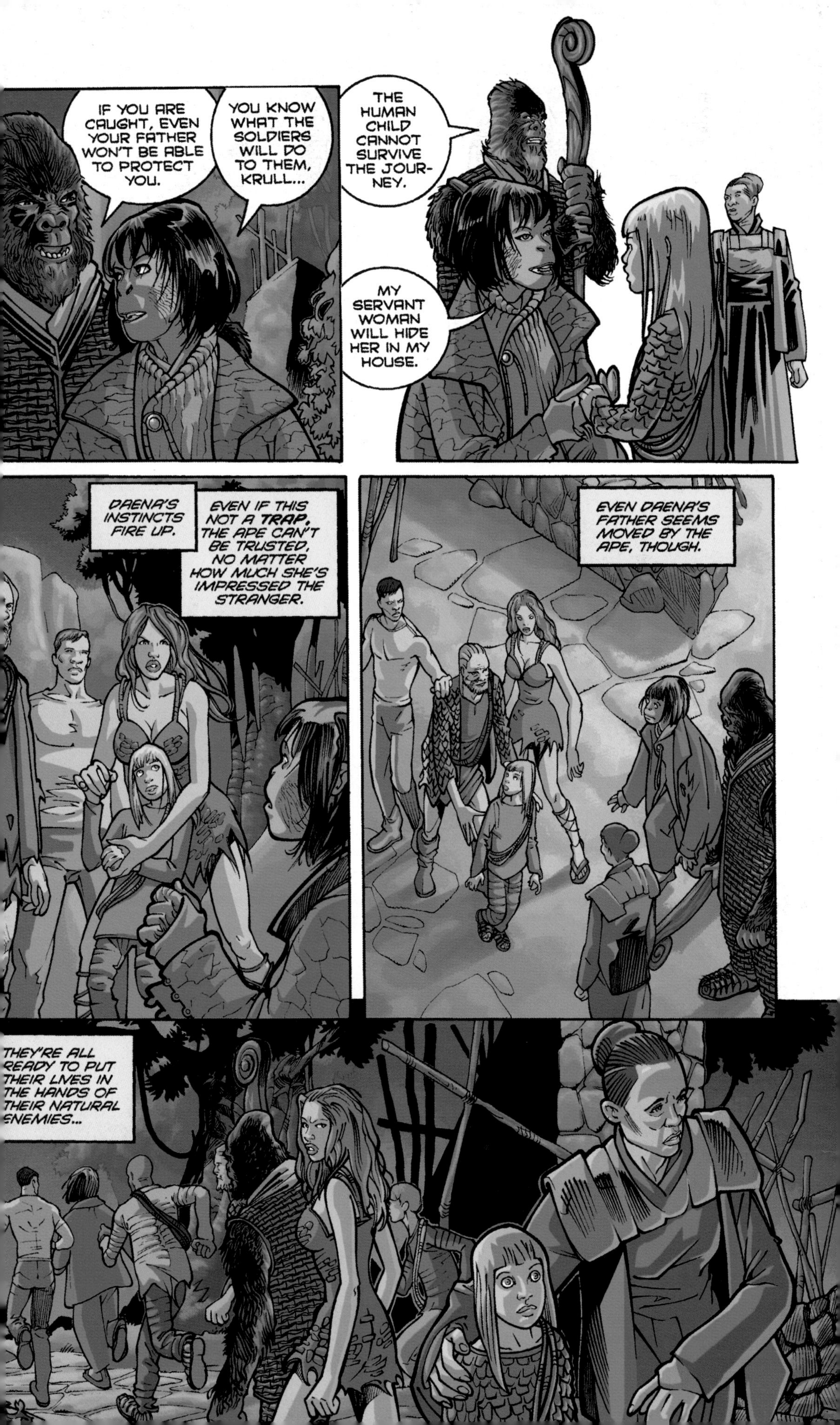

IF YOU ARE CAUGHT, EVEN YOUR FATHER WON'T BE ABLE TO PROTECT YOU.
YOU KNOW WHAT THE SOLDIERS WILL DO TO THEM, KRULL...
THE HUMAN CHILD CANNOT SURVIVE THE JOURNEY.
MY SERVANT WOMAN WILL HIDE HER IN MY HOUSE.
DAENA'S INSTINCTS FIRE UP.
EVEN IF THIS NOT A TRAP, THE APE CAN'T BE TRUSTED, NO MATTER HOW MUCH SHE'S IMPRESSED THE STRANGER.
EVEN DAENA'S FATHER SEEMS MOVED BY THE APE, THOUGH.
THEY'RE ALL READY TO PUT THEIR LIVES IN THE HANDS OF THEIR NATURAL ENEMIES...

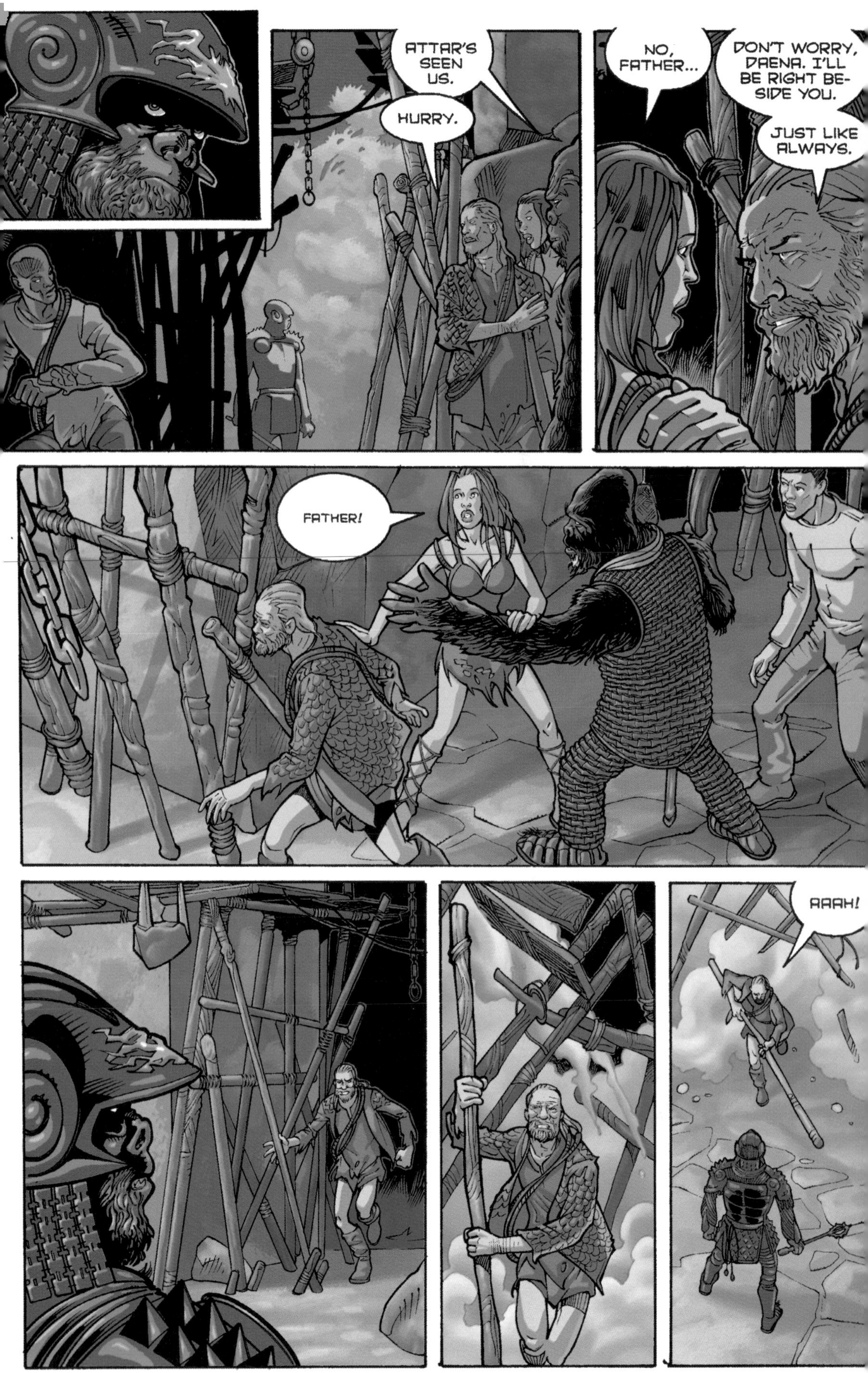
ATTAR'S SEEN US.
HURRY.
NO, FATHER...
DON'T WORRY, DAENA. I'LL BE RIGHT BE-SIDE YOU.
JUST LIKE ALWAYS.
FATHER!
AAAH!

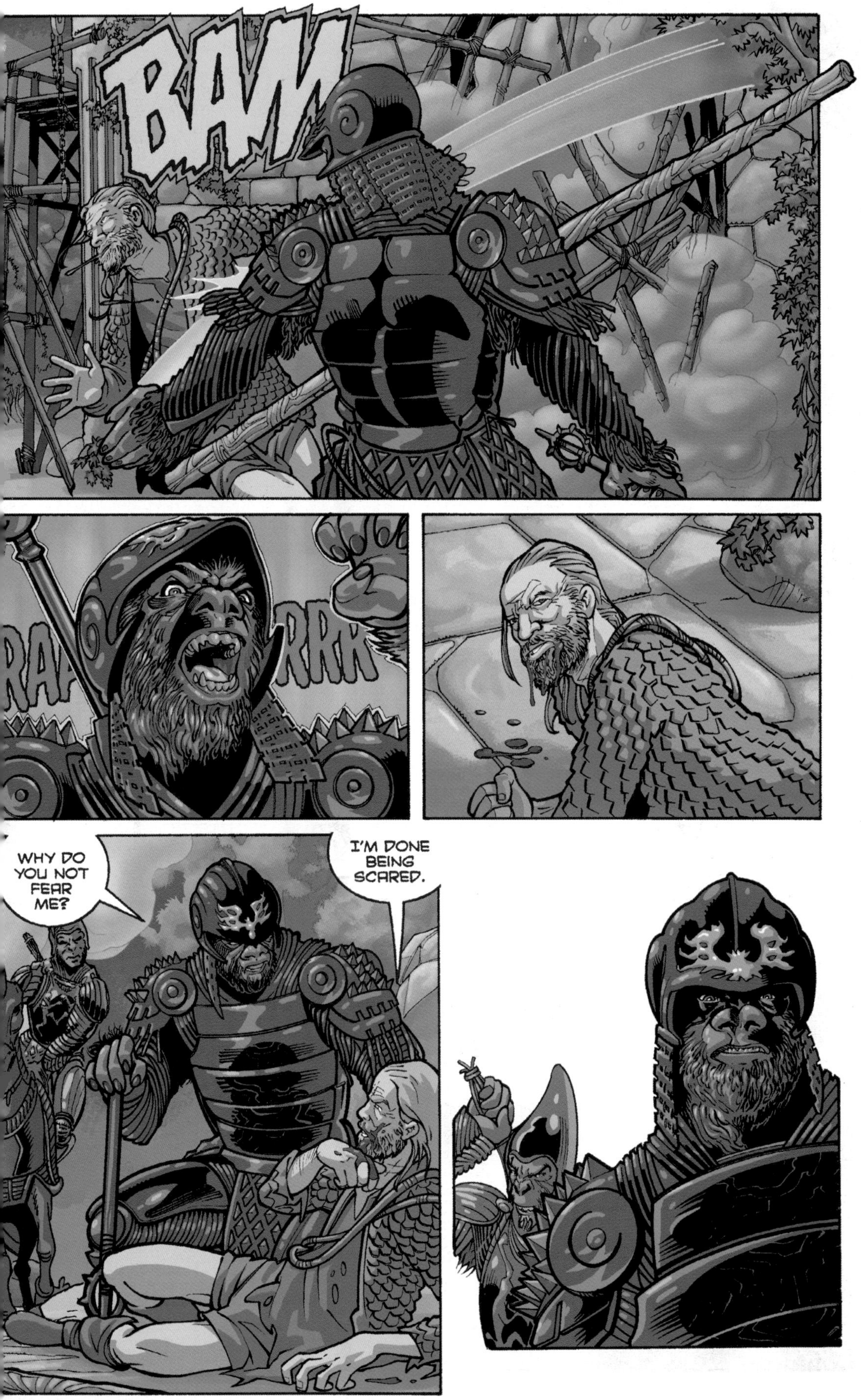
BAM
RAARRR
WHY DO YOU NOT FEAR ME?
I'M DONE BEING SCARED.

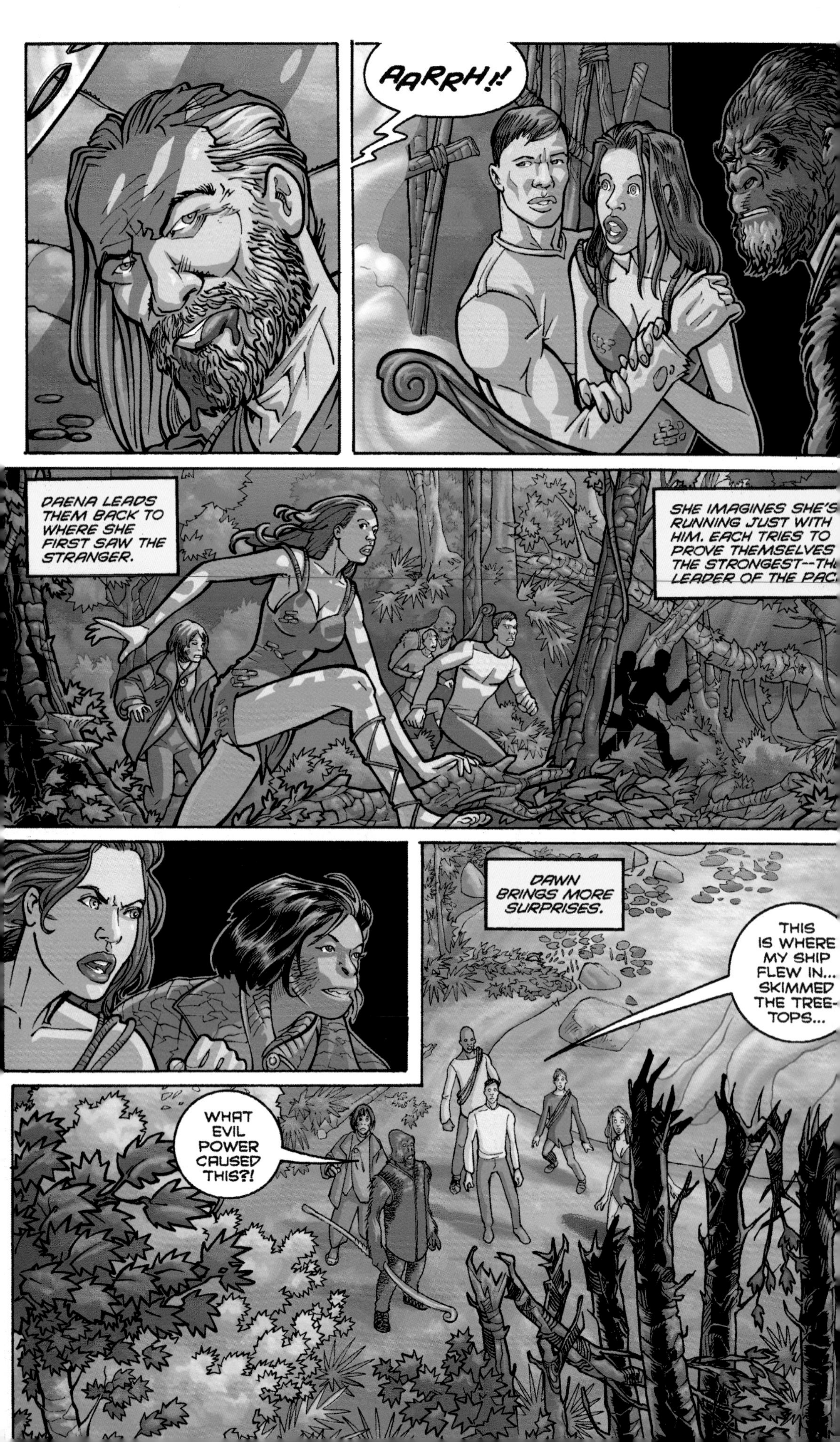
AARRH!!
DAENA LEADS THEM BACK TO WHERE SHE FIRST SAW THE STRANGER.
SHE IMAGINES SHE'S RUNNING JUST WITH HIM. EACH TRIES TO PROVE THEMSELVES THE STRONGEST--THE LEADER OF THE PAC
DAWN BRINGS MORE SURPRISES.
THIS IS WHERE MY SHIP FLEW IN... SKIMMED THE TREE-TOPS...
WHAT EVIL POWER CAUSED THIS?!

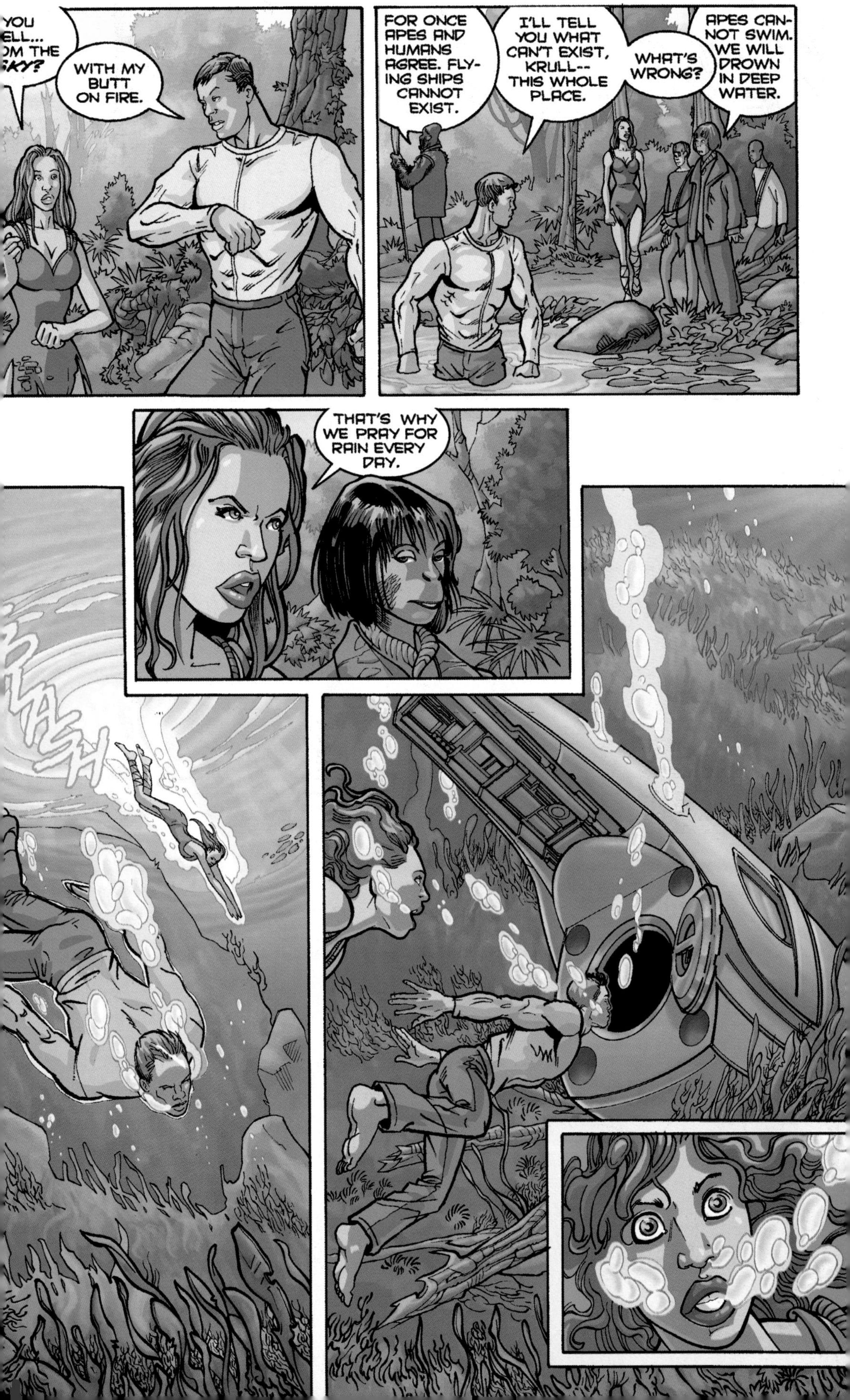

WITH MY BUTT ON FIRE.
FOR ONCE APES AND HUMANS AGREE. FLYING SHIPS CANNOT EXIST.
I'LL TELL YOU WHAT CAN'T EXIST, KRULL-- THIS WHOLE PLACE.
WHAT'S WRONG?
APES CANNOT SWIM. WE WILL DROWN IN DEEP WATER.
THAT'S WHY WE PRAY FOR RAIN EVERY DAY.

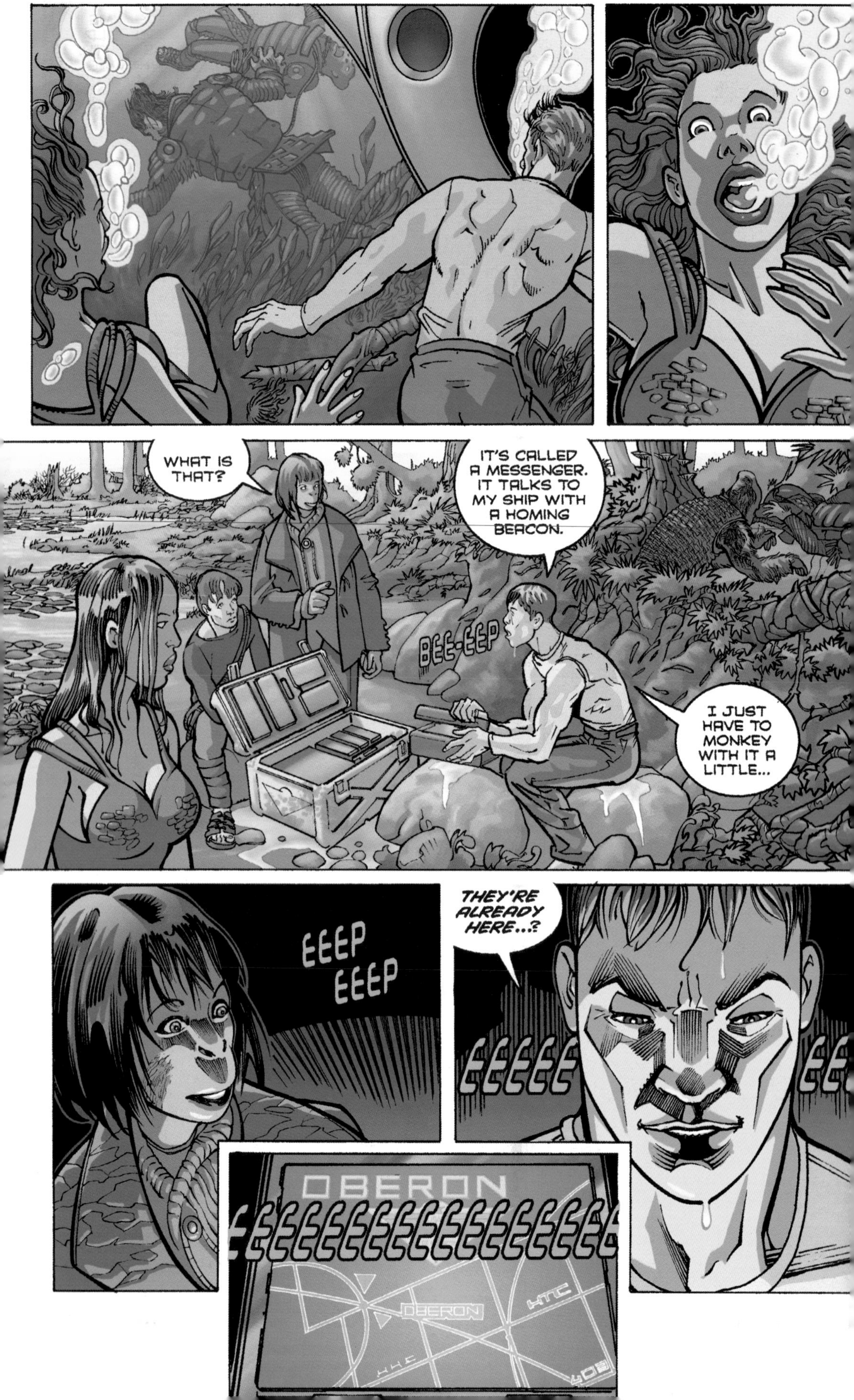
WHAT IS THAT?
IT'S CALLED A MESSENGER. IT TALKS TO MY SHIP WITH A HOMING BEACON.
BEE-EEP
I JUST HAVE TO MONKEY WITH IT A LITTLE...
EEEP EEEP
THEY'RE ALREADY HERE...?
EEEEE
OBERON
EEEEEEEEEEEEEEEEEEEEEEE
OBERON

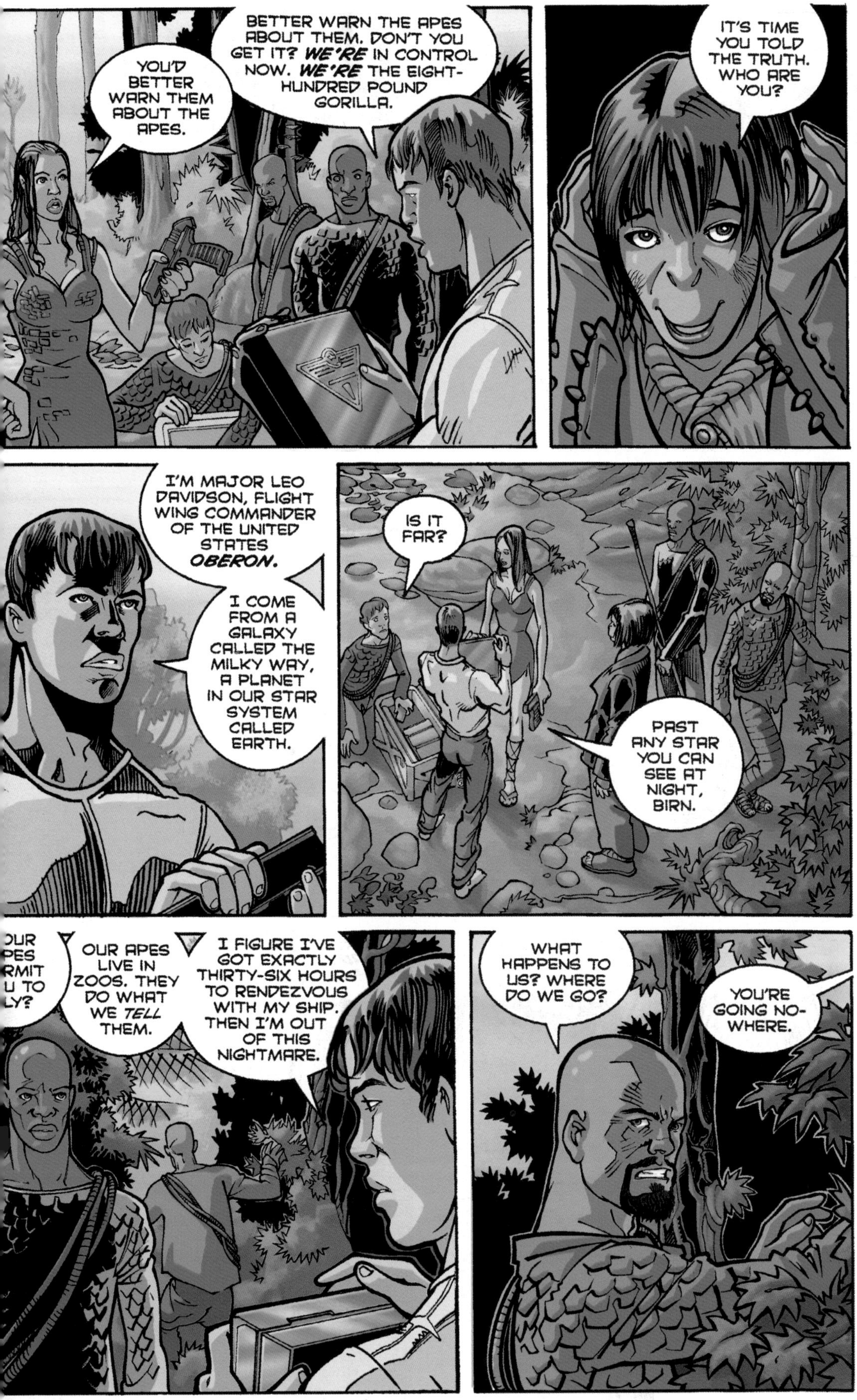
YOU'D BETTER WARN THEM ABOUT THE APES.
BETTER WARN THE APES ABOUT THEM. DON'T YOU GET IT? WE'RE IN CONTROL NOW. WE'RE THE EIGHT-HUNDRED POUND GORILLA.
IT'S TIME YOU TOLD THE TRUTH. WHO ARE YOU?
I'M MAJOR LEO DAVIDSON, FLIGHT WING COMMANDER OF THE UNITED STATES OBERON.
I COME FROM A GALAXY CALLED THE MILKY WAY, A PLANET IN OUR STAR SYSTEM CALLED EARTH.
IS IT FAR?
PAST ANY STAR YOU CAN SEE AT NIGHT, BIRN.
OUR APES LIVE IN ZOOS. THEY DO WHAT WE TELL THEM.
I FIGURE I'VE GOT EXACTLY THIRTY-SIX HOURS TO RENDEZVOUS WITH MY SHIP. THEN I'M OUT OF THIS NIGHTMARE.
WHAT HAPPENS TO US? WHERE DO WE GO?
YOU'RE GOING NO-WHERE.

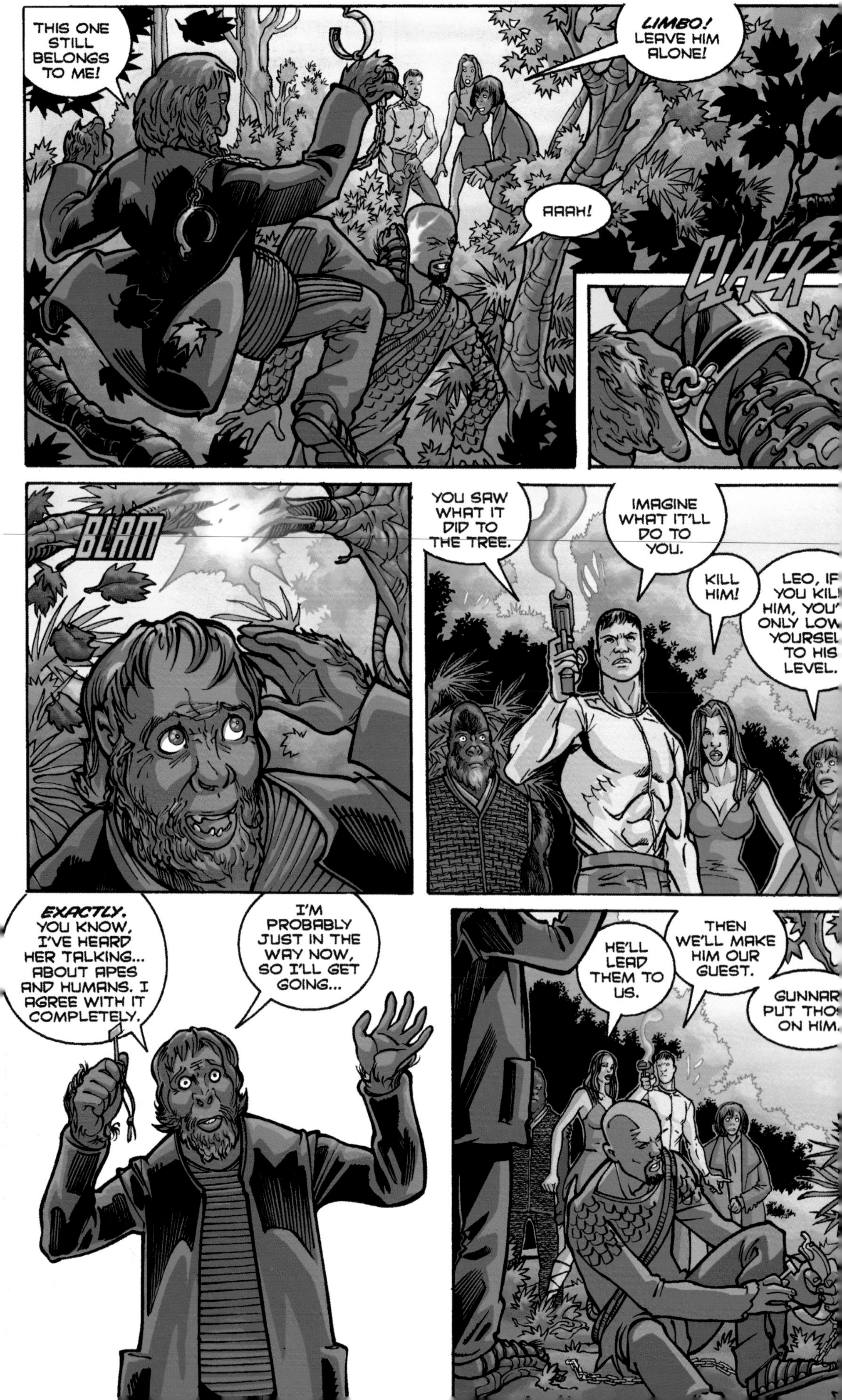

THIS ONE STILL BELONGS TO ME!
LIMBO! LEAVE HIM ALONE!
AAAH!
CLACK
BLAM
YOU SAW WHAT IT DID TO THE TREE.
IMAGINE WHAT IT'LL DO TO YOU.
KILL HIM!
LEO, IF YOU KIL HIM, YOU' ONLY LOW YOURSEL TO HIS LEVEL.
EXACTLY. YOU KNOW, I'VE HEARD HER TALKING... ABOUT APES AND HUMANS. I AGREE WITH IT COMPLETELY.
I'M PROBABLY JUST IN THE WAY NOW, SO I'LL GET GOING...
HE'LL LEAD THEM TO US.
THEN WE'LL MAKE HIM OUR GUEST.
GUNNAR PUT THO ON HIM.

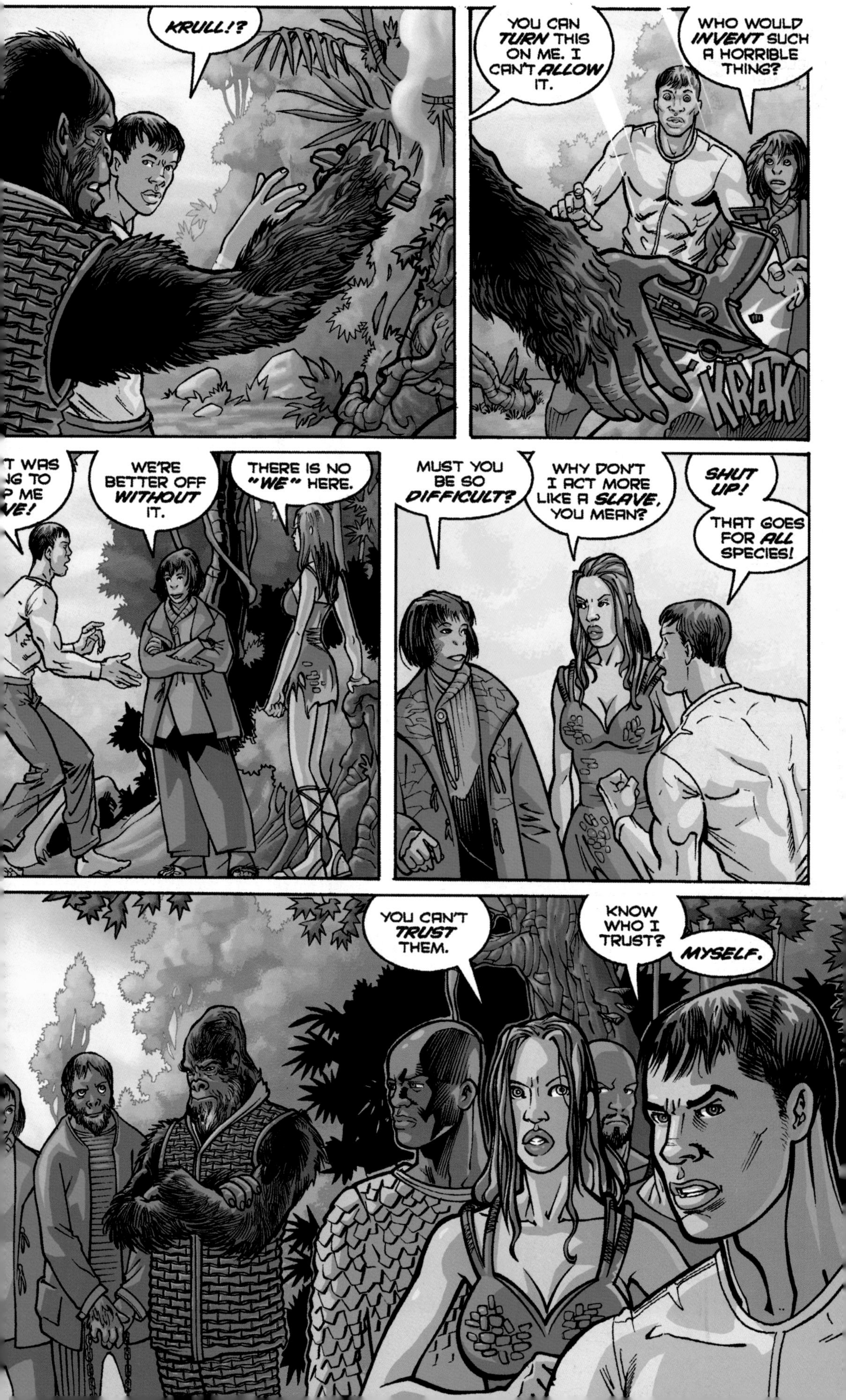
KRULL!?
YOU CAN TURN THIS ON ME. I CAN'T ALLOW IT.
WHO WOULD INVENT SUCH A HORRIBLE THING?
KRAK
WE'RE BETTER OFF WITHOUT IT.
THERE IS NO "WE" HERE.
MUST YOU BE SO DIFFICULT?
WHY DON'T I ACT MORE LIKE A SLAVE, YOU MEAN?
SHUT UP!
THAT GOES FOR ALL SPECIES!
YOU CAN'T TRUST THEM.
KNOW WHO I TRUST?
MYSELF.

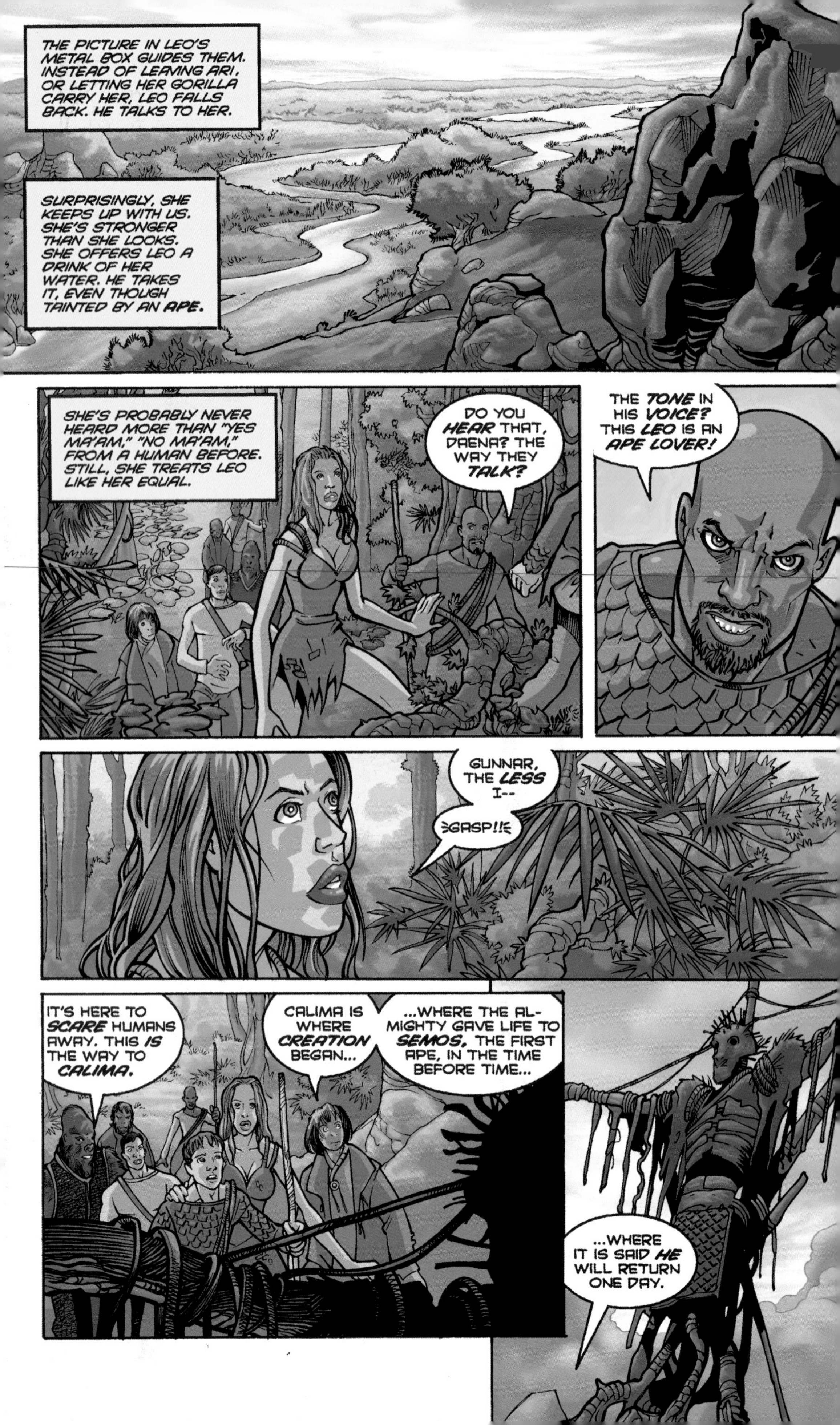
THE PICTURE IN LEO'S METAL BOX GUIDES THEM. INSTEAD OF LEAVING ARI, OR LETTING HER GORILLA CARRY HER, LEO FALLS BACK. HE TALKS TO HER.
SURPRISINGLY, SHE KEEPS UP WITH US. SHE'S STRONGER THAN SHE LOOKS. SHE OFFERS LEO A DRINK OF HER WATER. HE TAKES IT, EVEN THOUGH TAINTED BY AN *APE*.
SHE'S PROBABLY NEVER HEARD MORE THAN "YES MA'AM," "NO MA'AM," FROM A HUMAN BEFORE. STILL, SHE TREATS LEO LIKE HER EQUAL.
DO YOU *HEAR* THAT, DAENA? THE WAY THEY *TALK?*
THE *TONE* IN HIS *VOICE?* THIS *LEO* IS AN *APE LOVER!*
GUNNAR, THE *LESS* I--
GASP!!
IT'S HERE TO *SCARE* HUMANS AWAY. THIS *IS* THE WAY TO *CALIMA.*
CALIMA IS WHERE *CREATION* BEGAN...
...WHERE THE AL-MIGHTY GAVE LIFE TO *SEMOS,* THE FIRST APE, IN THE TIME BEFORE TIME...
...WHERE IT IS SAID *HE* WILL RETURN ONE DAY.

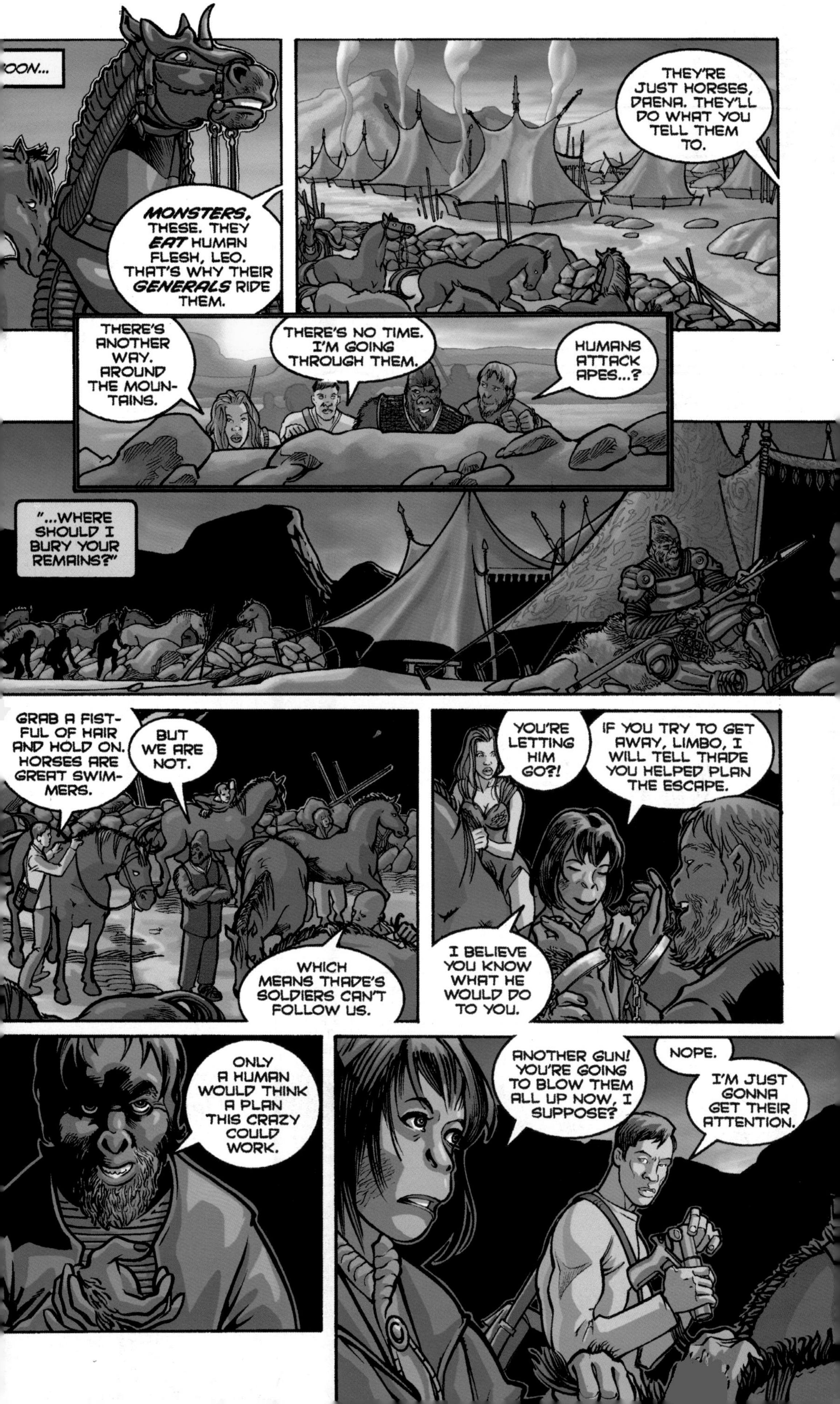
OON...
MONSTERS, THESE. THEY EAT HUMAN FLESH, LEO. THAT'S WHY THEIR GENERALS RIDE THEM.
THEY'RE JUST HORSES, DAENA. THEY'LL DO WHAT YOU TELL THEM TO.
THERE'S ANOTHER WAY. AROUND THE MOUNTAINS.
THERE'S NO TIME. I'M GOING THROUGH THEM.
HUMANS ATTACK APES...?
"...WHERE SHOULD I BURY YOUR REMAINS?"
GRAB A FISTFUL OF HAIR AND HOLD ON. HORSES ARE GREAT SWIMMERS.
BUT WE ARE NOT.
WHICH MEANS THADE'S SOLDIERS CAN'T FOLLOW US.
YOU'RE LETTING HIM GO?!
IF YOU TRY TO GET AWAY, LIMBO, I WILL TELL THADE YOU HELPED PLAN THE ESCAPE.
I BELIEVE YOU KNOW WHAT HE WOULD DO TO YOU.
ONLY A HUMAN WOULD THINK A PLAN THIS CRAZY COULD WORK.
ANOTHER GUN! YOU'RE GOING TO BLOW THEM ALL UP NOW, I SUPPOSE?
NOPE.
I'M JUST GONNA GET THEIR ATTENTION.

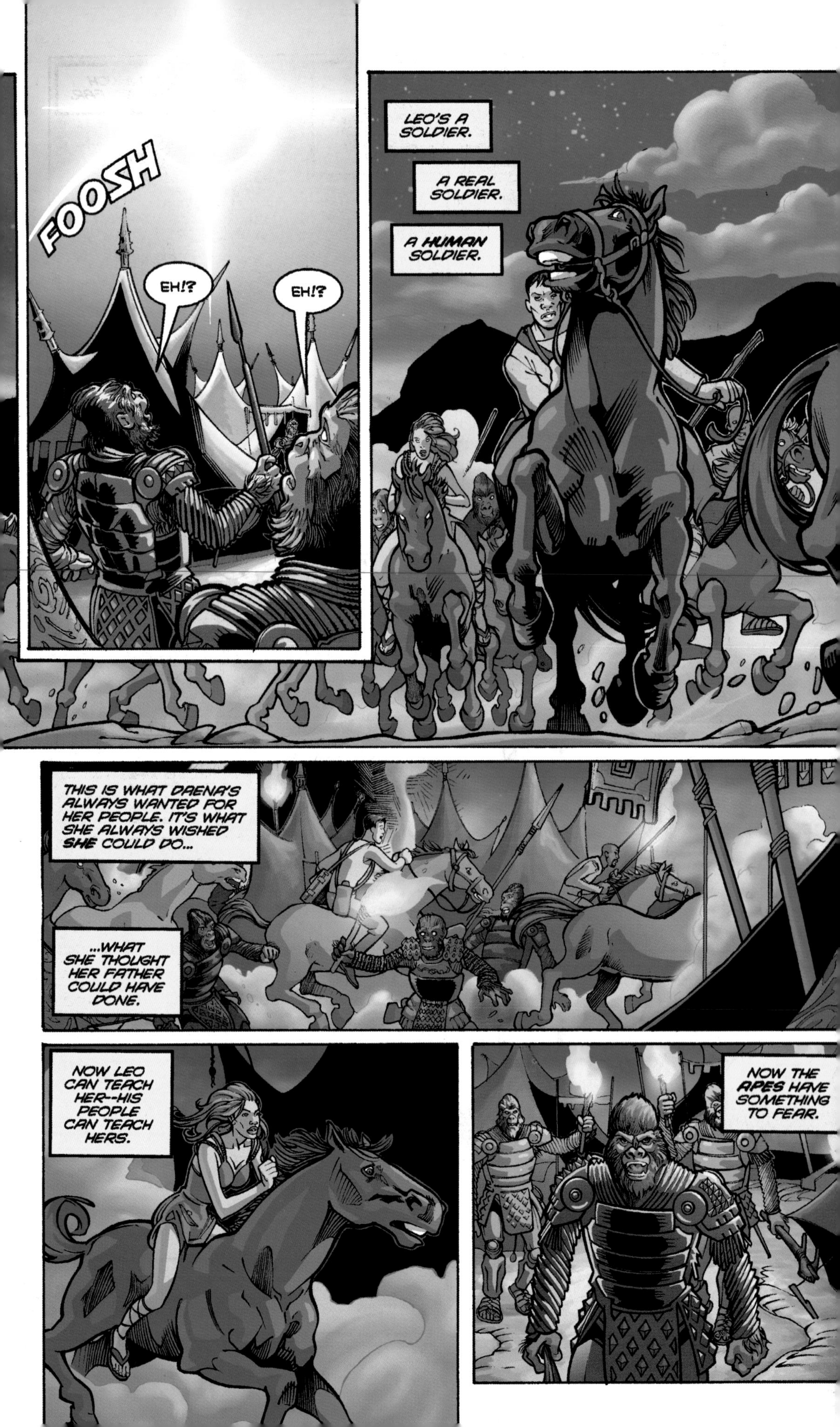
FOOSH
EH!?
EH!?
LEO'S A SOLDIER.
A REAL SOLDIER.
A HUMAN SOLDIER.
THIS IS WHAT DAENA'S ALWAYS WANTED FOR HER PEOPLE. IT'S WHAT SHE ALWAYS WISHED SHE COULD DO...
...WHAT SHE THOUGHT HER FATHER COULD HAVE DONE.
NOW LEO CAN TEACH HER--HIS PEOPLE CAN TEACH HERS.
NOW THE APES HAVE SOMETHING TO FEAR.

'S IRONIC AT DAENA THOUGHT ORSES EAT MAN FLESH, CE ARI HER- F IS HAVING FAR MORE IFFICULT E THAN ANY OF THEM.

THEN HER HORSE STUMBLES, TAKEN DOWN BY ONE OF HER OWN KIND.

ARI'S RUN SO MUCH TODAY, COME SO FAR.

OKING TOWARD WATER, WITH TAR RUNNING BEHIND HER, URDER IN HIS S, SHE'S SUD- NLY SURE OF OMETHING.

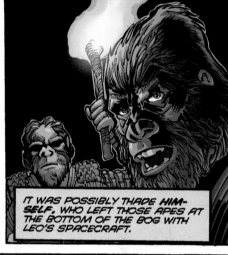

IT WAS POSSIBLY THADE HIM- SELF, WHO LEFT THOSE APES AT THE BOTTOM OF THE BOG WITH LEO'S SPACECRAFT.

SWIM!

I CAN'T!

I WON'T LET GO!

SHE HEARS ATTAR'S HOWL OF FAILURE...

...AND THEN SHE HEARS ONLY HER OWN BLOOD, POUNDING IN HER EARS.

THEY DIDN'T MAKE IT.

WAIT, THERE'S NO NEED NOW--THEY TRIED TO KILL ME! LIKE I WAS NOTHING BUT A MISERABLE--

HUMAN?

THERE ARE OTHERS IN THE HILLS THAT FIGHT APES. WE SHOULD JOIN THEM.

WE SHOULD STAY TOGETHER, GUNNAR.

WE SHOULD STICK TO OUR OWN KIND!

NOTHING WILL EVER CHANGE...

LEO!?

THERE ARE SCRATCHES ON LEO'S SHOULDERS FROM THE SHE-APE'S CLAWS, BUT DAENA KNOWS SHE DIDN'T WANT TO HURT HIM.

SHE WAS HOLDING ON.

DAENA ALSO KNOWS THAT THIS SHE-APE WANTS MORE FROM LEO THAN A RESCUE.

THEY'LL HEAD DOW[N] RIVER UN[TIL] THEY FIN[D] A CROSS[S]ING.

WE SHOULD KEEP MOVING.

YOU RECOVERED QUICK.

THEY'RE NOT HERE.

BEEP BEEP

BEEP BEEP BEEP

THEY WERE NEVER HERE.

BEEP BEEP

I KNOW THIS SMELL... RIGHT, IT'S A CATAS-TROPHE...

BEEP

BEEP BEEP

NO... NO...

BEEP

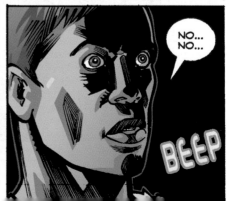

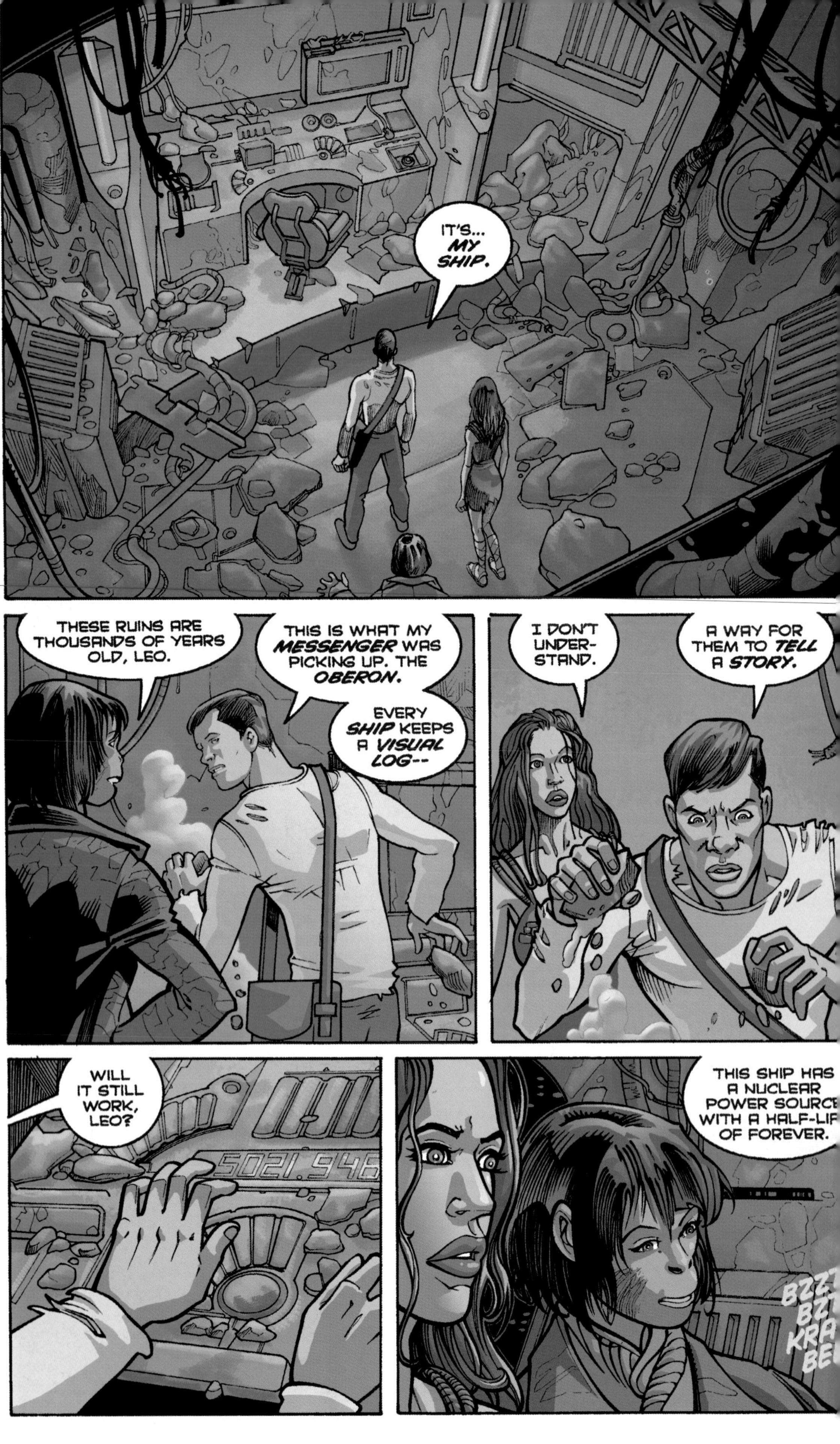
IT'S... MY SHIP.
THESE RUINS ARE THOUSANDS OF YEARS OLD, LEO.
THIS IS WHAT MY MESSENGER WAS PICKING UP. THE OBERON.
EVERY SHIP KEEPS A VISUAL LOG--
I DON'T UNDER-STAND.
A WAY FOR THEM TO TELL A STORY.
WILL IT STILL WORK, LEO?
5021.946
THIS SHIP HAS A NUCLEAR POWER SOURCE WITH A HALF-LIFE OF FOREVER.

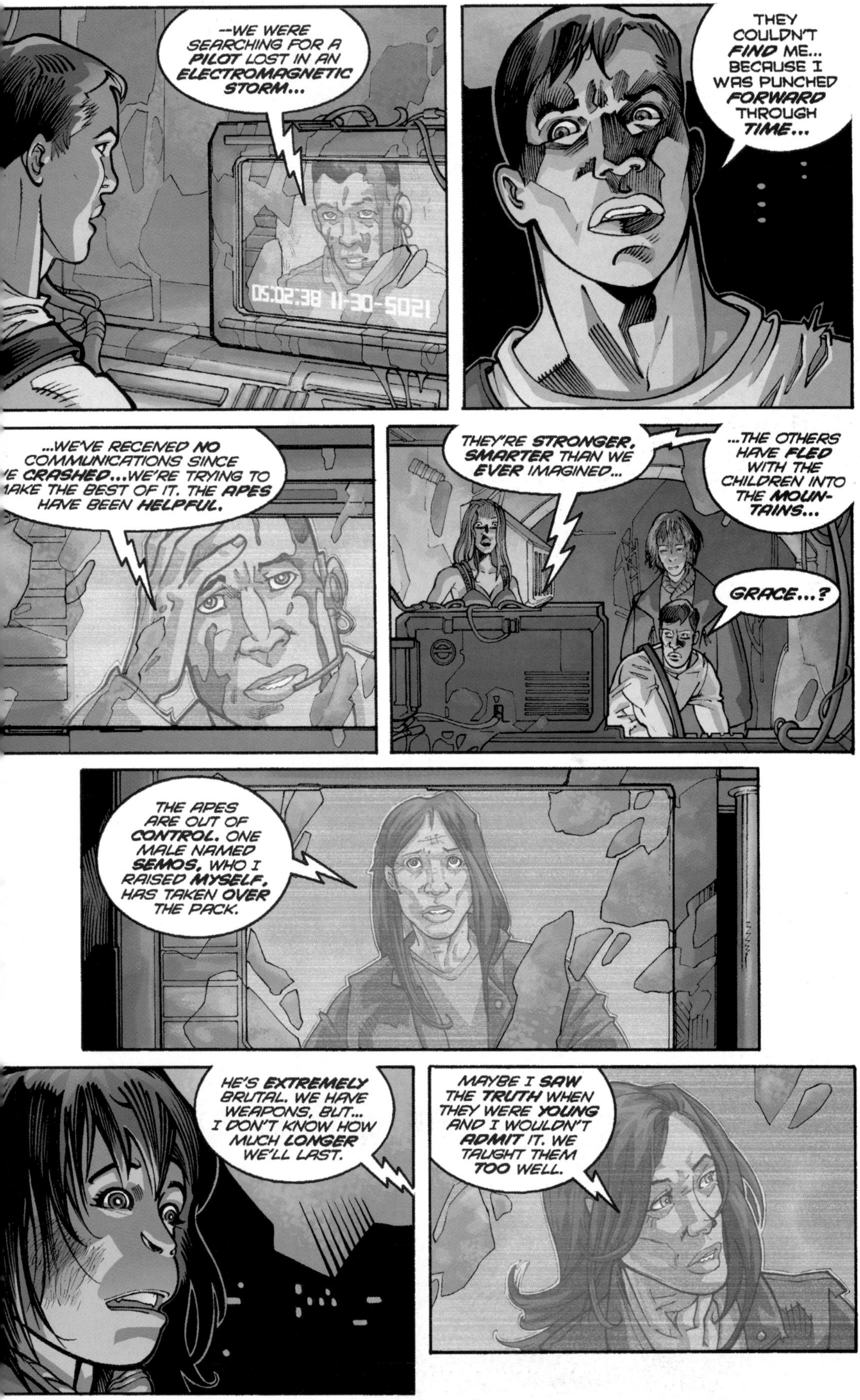
--WE WERE SEARCHING FOR A PILOT LOST IN AN ELECTROMAGNETIC STORM...
05:02:38 11-30-5021
THEY COULDN'T FIND ME... BECAUSE I WAS PUNCHED FORWARD THROUGH TIME...
...WE'VE RECEIVED NO COMMUNICATIONS SINCE WE CRASHED...WE'RE TRYING TO MAKE THE BEST OF IT. THE APES HAVE BEEN HELPFUL.
THEY'RE STRONGER, SMARTER THAN WE EVER IMAGINED...
...THE OTHERS HAVE FLED WITH THE CHILDREN INTO THE MOUNTAINS...
GRACE...?
THE APES ARE OUT OF CONTROL. ONE MALE NAMED SEMOS, WHO I RAISED MYSELF, HAS TAKEN OVER THE PACK.
HE'S EXTREMELY BRUTAL. WE HAVE WEAPONS, BUT... I DON'T KNOW HOW MUCH LONGER WE'LL LAST.
MAYBE I SAW THE TRUTH WHEN THEY WERE YOUNG AND I WOULDN'T ADMIT IT. WE TAUGHT THEM TOO WELL.

THEY WERE *APT* PUPILS--

AAAHH!

KSSH

CRACKL

tz-tz-tz

SMASH!

ZZT-KK!

SSSHH-

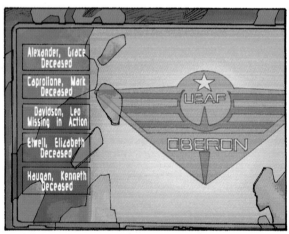

Alexander, Grace
Deceased

Caprallone, Mark
Deceased

Davidson, Leo
Missing in Action

Etwell, Elizabeth
Deceased

Haugen, Kenneth
Deceased

USAF

OBERON

THE CRAS
THEIR *DEATH*
THEY'RE AL
DEAD BECA
THEY W
LOOKING F
ME...

BUT WE'RE ALL *ALIVE* BECAUSE OF YOU.

THERE'S A LITTLE *POWER* LEFT IN ONE OF THE *FUEL RODS*.

YOU'RE TRYING TO FIND A WAY TO *LEAVE* US...!

I'VE BEEN AWAY FROM MY HOME A *THOUSAND* YEARS!

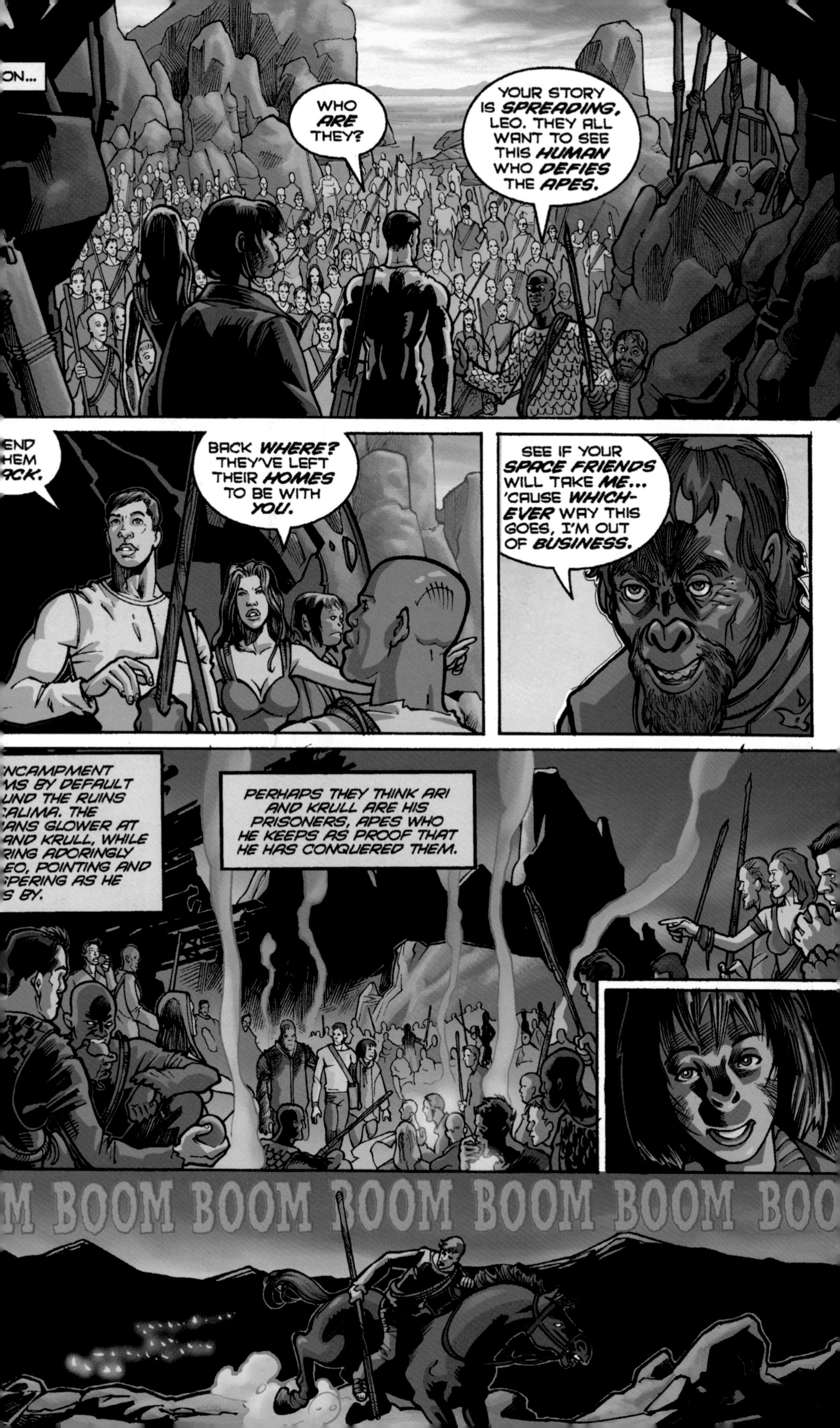
ON...
WHO ARE THEY?
YOUR STORY IS SPREADING, LEO. THEY ALL WANT TO SEE THIS HUMAN WHO DEFIES THE APES.
END HEM ACK.
BACK WHERE? THEY'VE LEFT THEIR HOMES TO BE WITH YOU.
SEE IF YOUR SPACE FRIENDS WILL TAKE ME... 'CAUSE WHICH-EVER WAY THIS GOES, I'M OUT OF BUSINESS.
NCAMPMENT MS BY DEFAULT UND THE RUINS CALIMA. THE ANS GLOWER AT AND KRULL, WHILE RING ADORINGLY EO, POINTING AND PERING AS HE S BY.
PERHAPS THEY THINK ARI AND KRULL ARE HIS PRISONERS, APES WHO HE KEEPS AS PROOF THAT HE HAS CONQUERED THEM.
M BOOM BOOM BOOM BOOM BOOM BOO

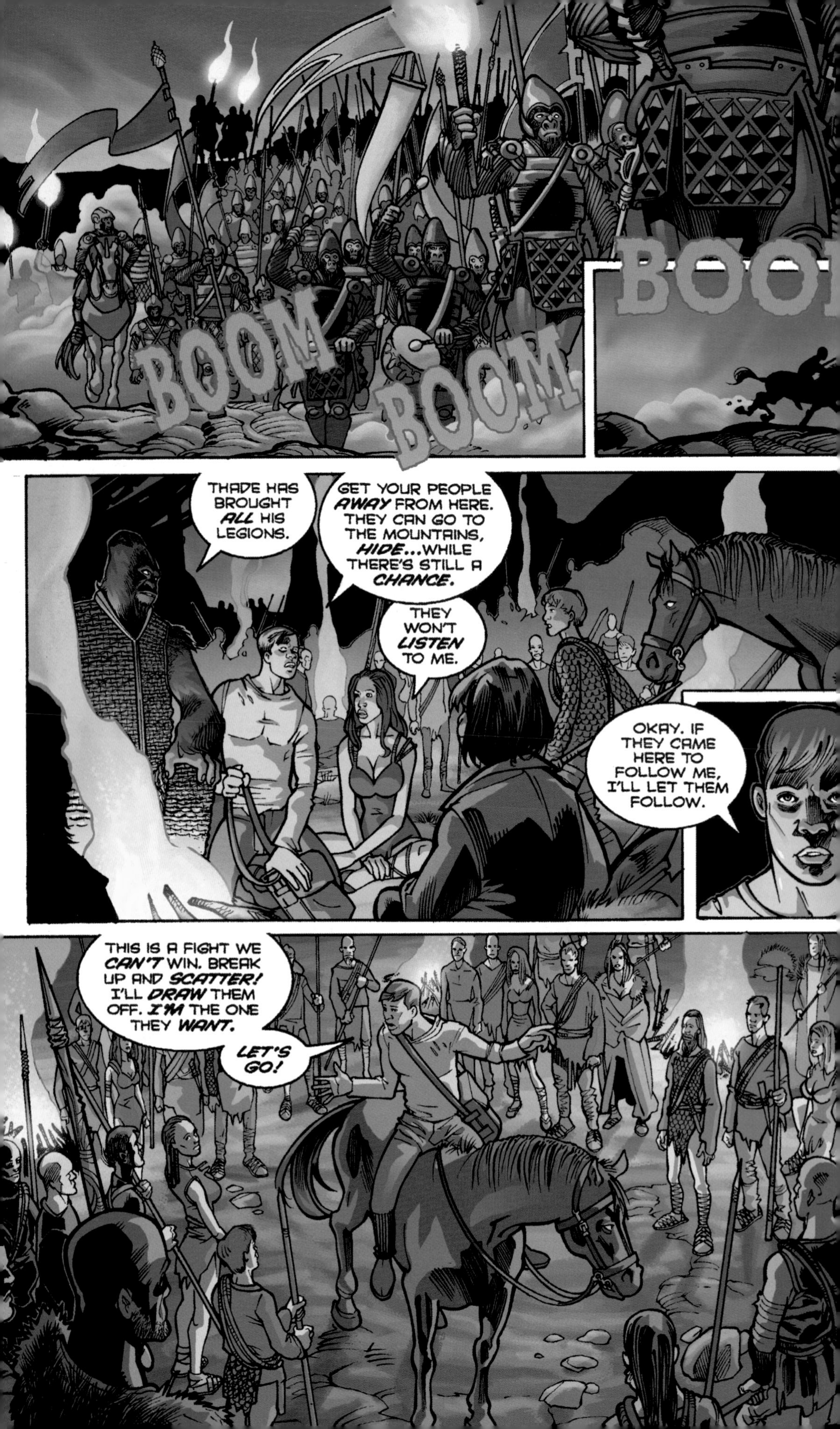
BOOM
BOOM
BOOM
THADE HAS BROUGHT ALL HIS LEGIONS.
GET YOUR PEOPLE AWAY FROM HERE. THEY CAN GO TO THE MOUNTAINS, HIDE...WHILE THERE'S STILL A CHANCE.
THEY WON'T LISTEN TO ME.
OKAY. IF THEY CAME HERE TO FOLLOW ME, I'LL LET THEM FOLLOW.
THIS IS A FIGHT WE CAN'T WIN. BREAK UP AND SCATTER! I'LL DRAW THEM OFF. I'M THE ONE THEY WANT.
LET'S GO!

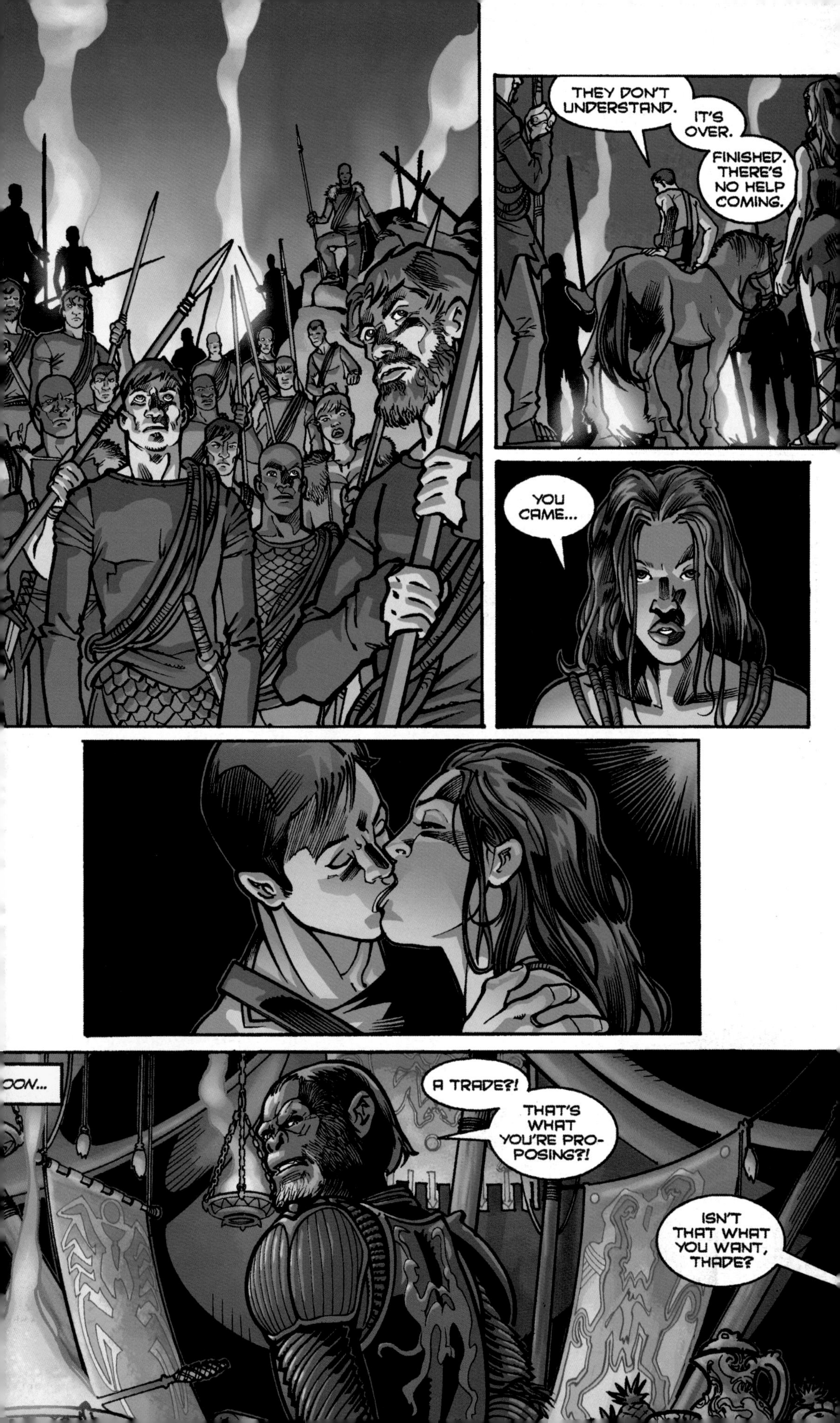
THEY DON'T UNDERSTAND.
IT'S OVER.
FINISHED. THERE'S NO HELP COMING.
YOU CAME...
OON...
A TRADE?!
THAT'S WHAT YOU'RE PRO-POSING?!
ISN'T THAT WHAT YOU WANT, THADE?

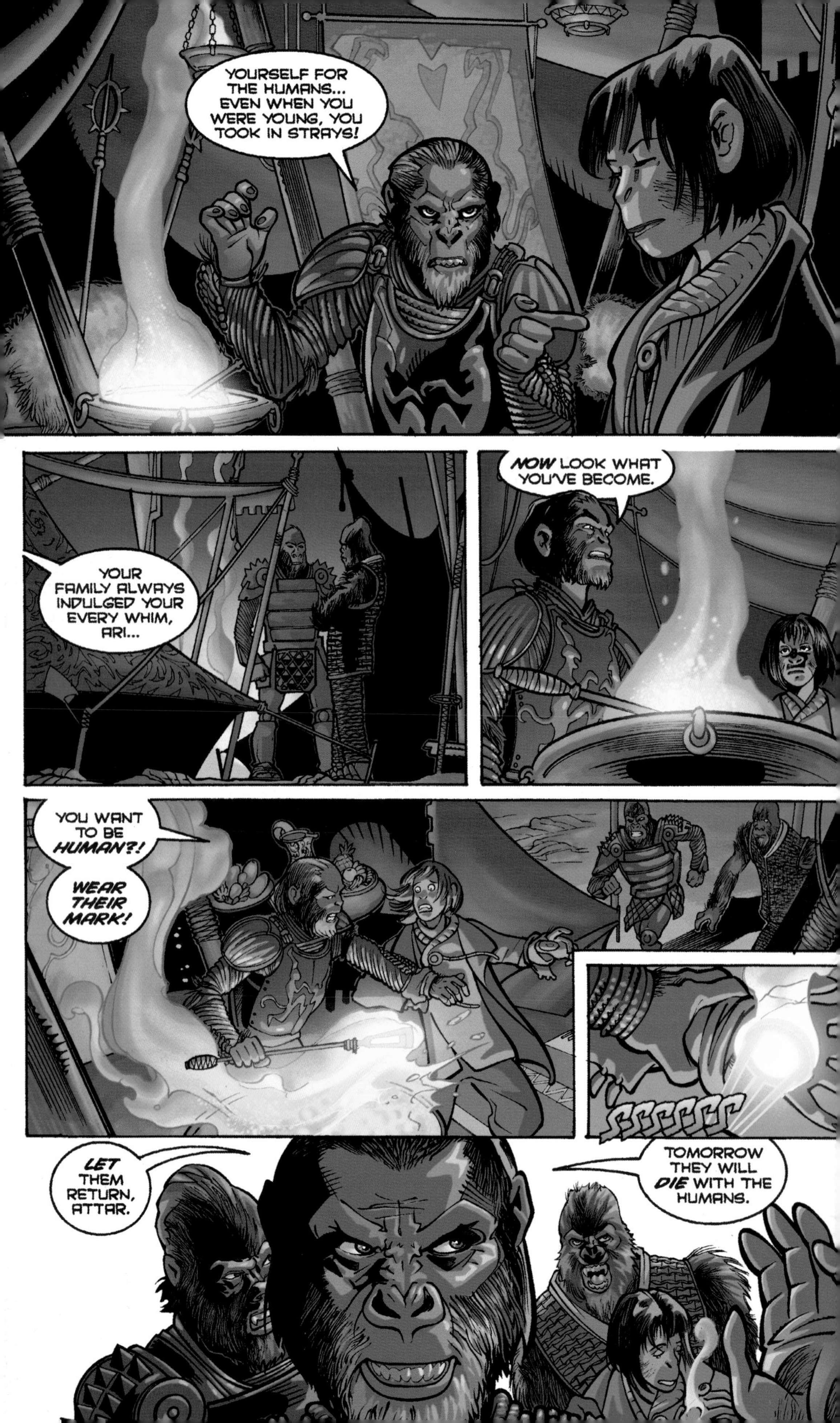
YOURSELF FOR THE HUMANS... EVEN WHEN YOU WERE YOUNG, YOU TOOK IN STRAYS!
YOUR FAMILY ALWAYS INDULGED YOUR EVERY WHIM, ARI...
NOW LOOK WHAT YOU'VE BECOME.
YOU WANT TO BE HUMAN?!
WEAR THEIR MARK!
SSSSSS
LET THEM RETURN, ATTAR.
TOMORROW THEY WILL DIE WITH THE HUMANS.

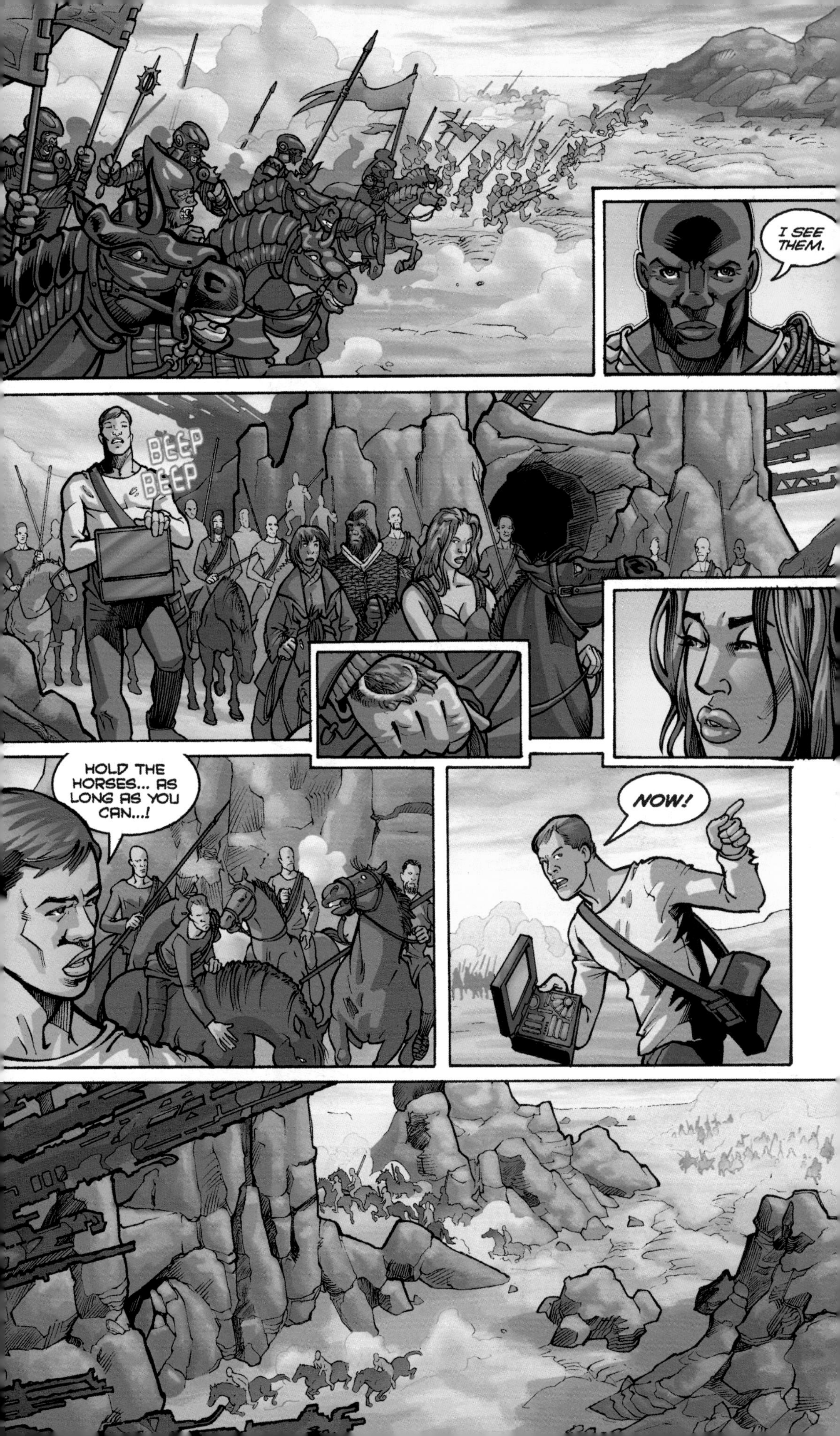
I SEE THEM.
BEEP BEEP
HOLD THE HORSES... AS LONG AS YOU CAN...!
NOW!

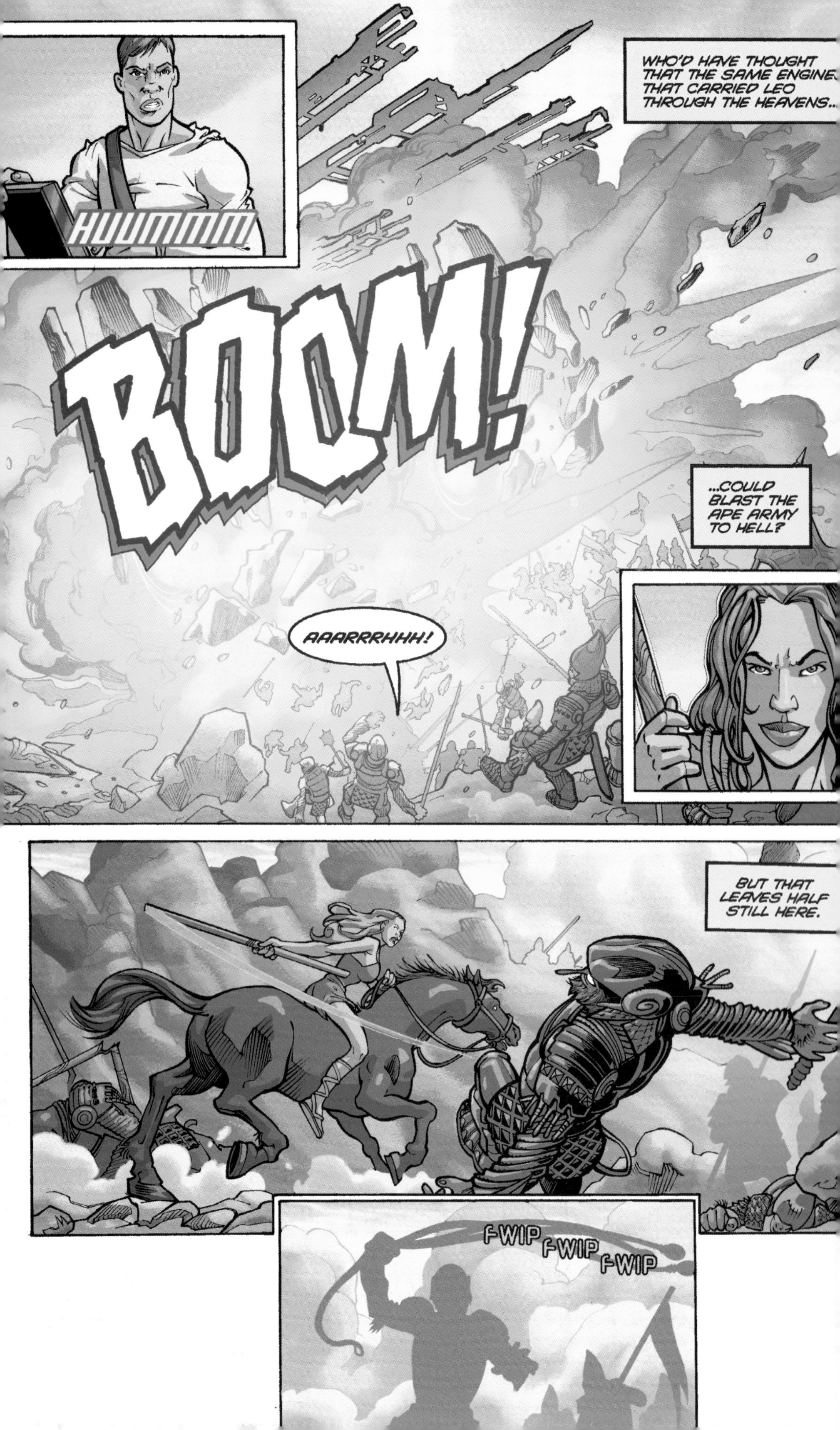
HUUMMM
WHO'D HAVE THOUGHT THAT THE SAME ENGINE THAT CARRIED LEO THROUGH THE HEAVENS...
BOOM!
...COULD BLAST THE APE ARMY TO HELL?
AAARRRHHH!
BUT THAT LEAVES HALF STILL HERE.
FWIP FWIP FWIP

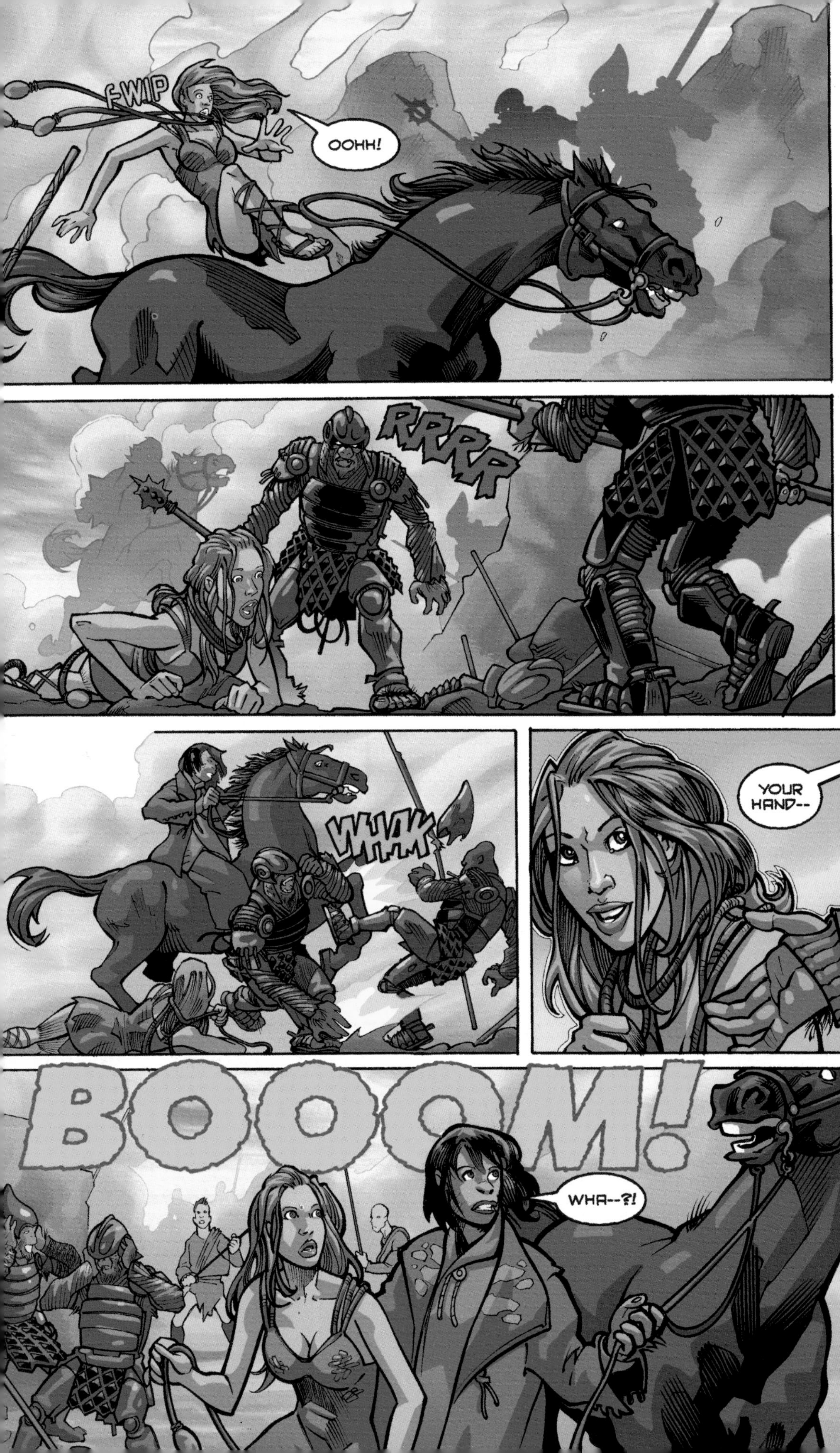
FWIP
OOHH!
RRRR
WHAK
YOUR HAND--
BOOOM!
WHA--?!

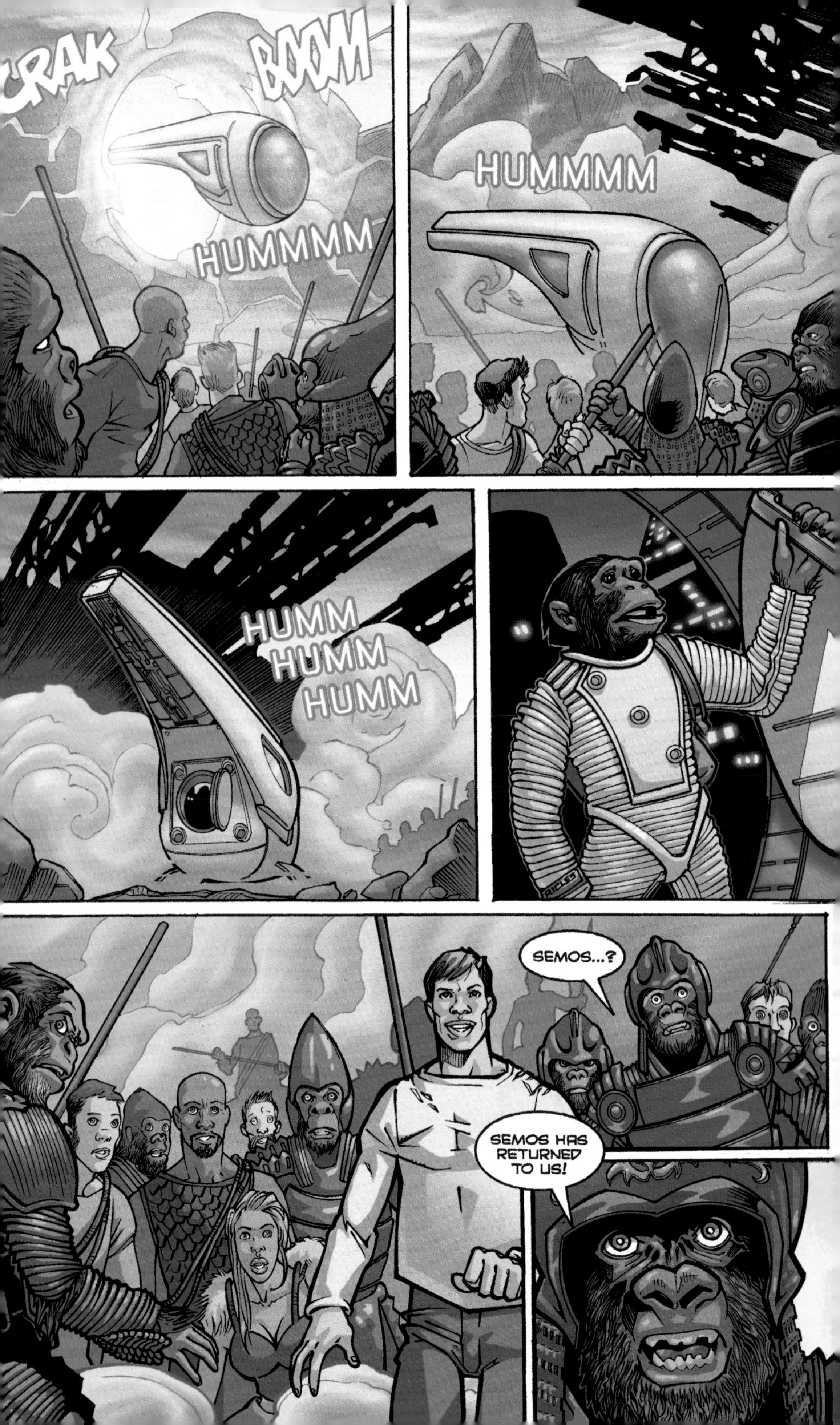

CRAK
BOOM
HUMMMM
HUMMMM
HUMM
HUMM
HUMM
SEMOS...?
SEMOS HAS RETURNED TO US!

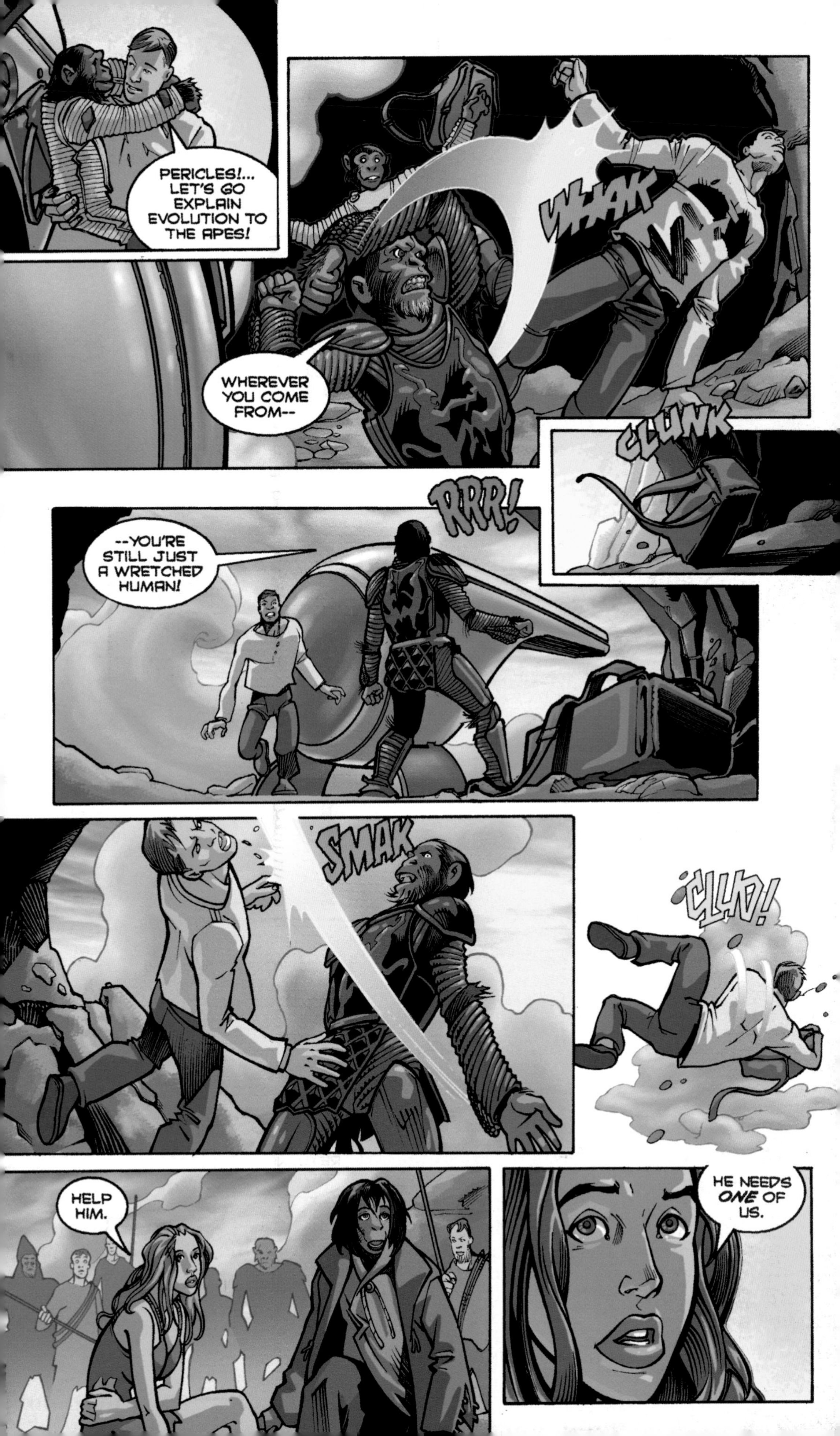

PERICLES!... LET'S GO EXPLAIN EVOLUTION TO THE APES!
WHAK
WHEREVER YOU COME FROM--
CLUNK
RRR!
--YOU'RE STILL JUST A WRETCHED HUMAN!
SMAK
CLUD!
HELP HIM.
HE NEEDS *ONE* OF US.

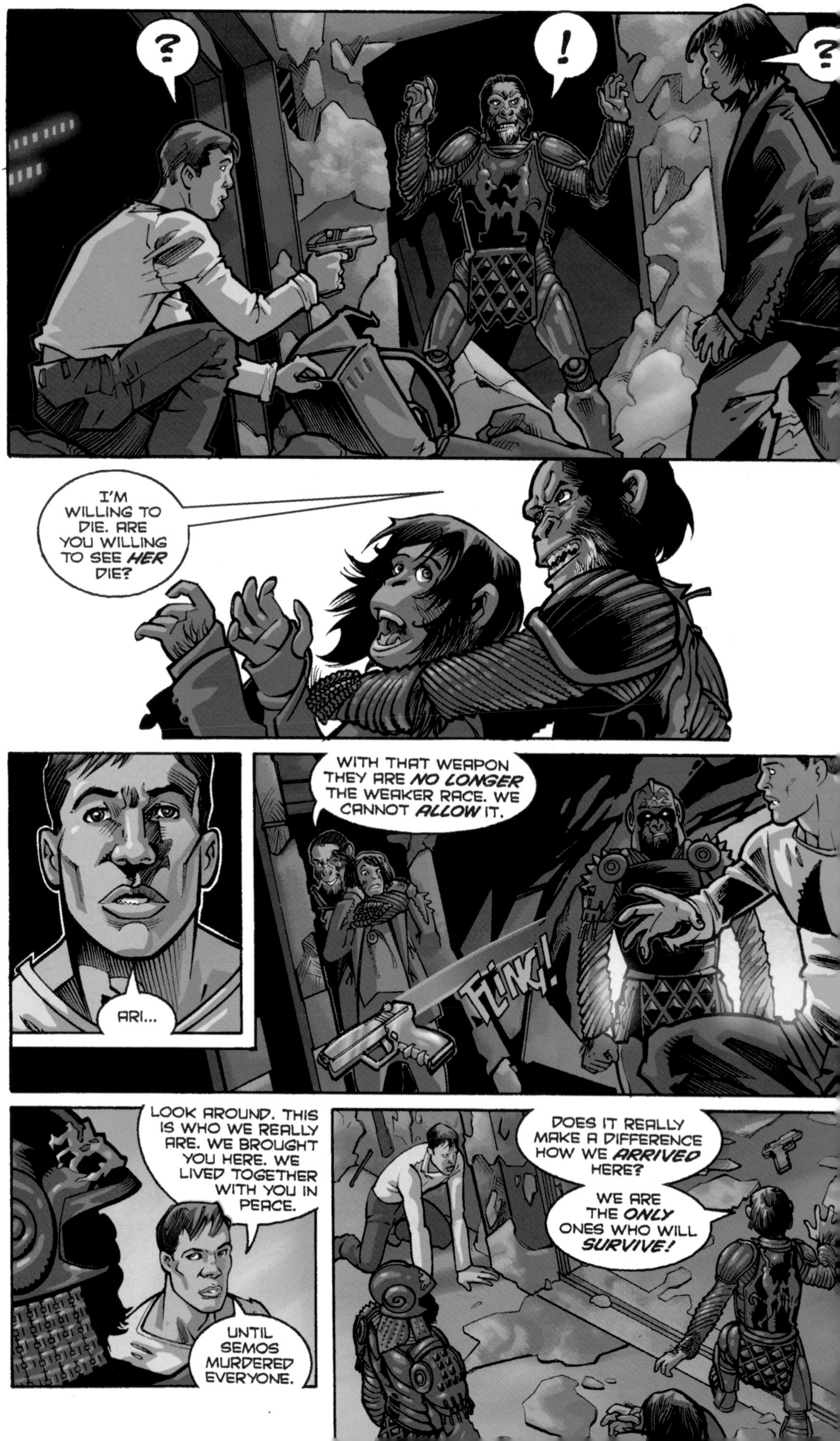
?
!
?
I'M WILLING TO DIE. ARE YOU WILLING TO SEE *HER* DIE?
ARI...
WITH THAT WEAPON THEY ARE *NO LONGER* THE WEAKER RACE. WE CANNOT *ALLOW* IT.
FLING!
LOOK AROUND. THIS IS WHO WE REALLY ARE. WE BROUGHT YOU HERE. WE LIVED TOGETHER WITH YOU IN PEACE.
UNTIL SEMOS MURDERED EVERYONE.
DOES IT REALLY MAKE A DIFFERENCE HOW WE *ARRIVED* HERE?
WE ARE THE *ONLY* ONES WHO WILL *SURVIVE!*

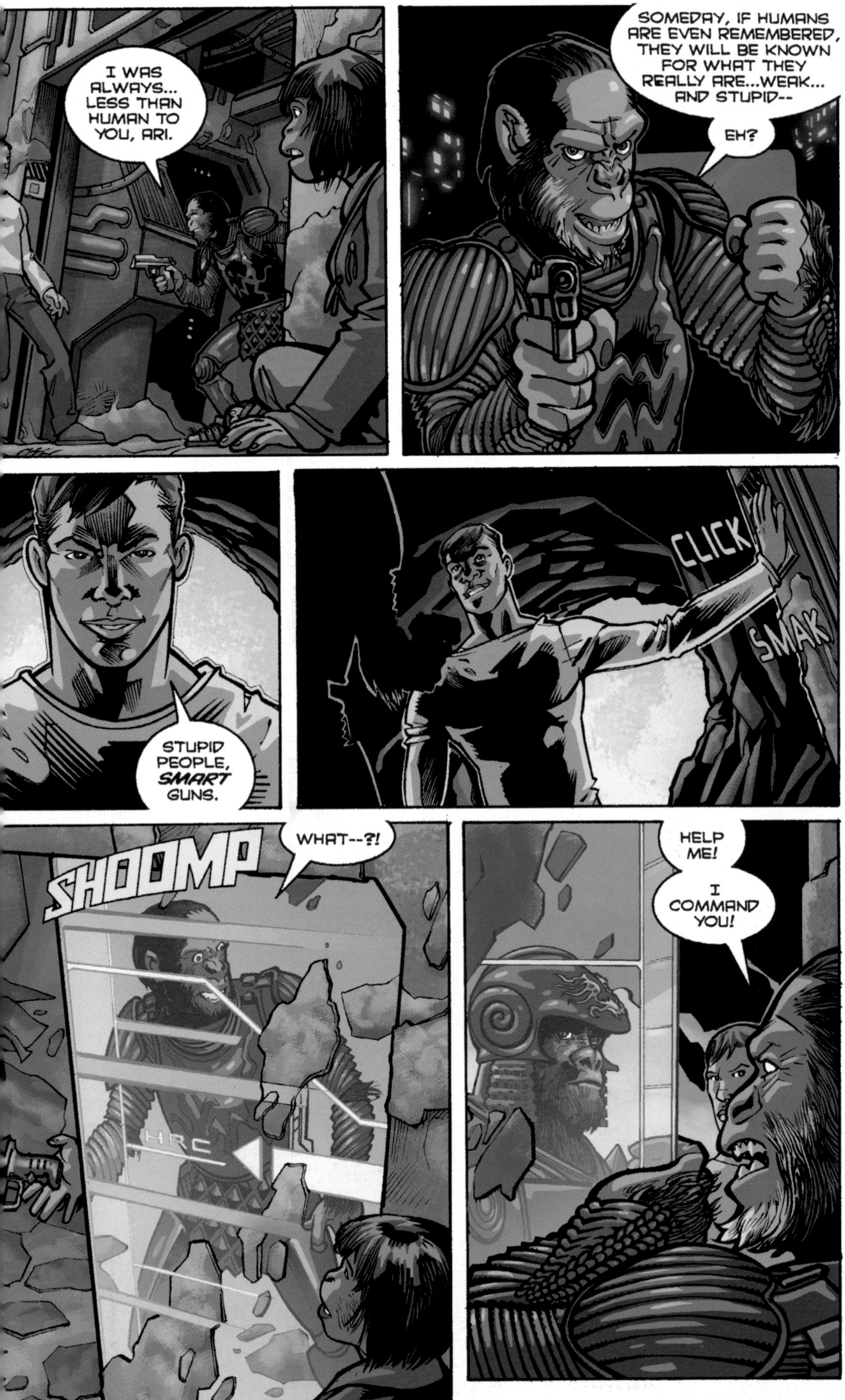
I WAS ALWAYS... LESS THAN HUMAN TO YOU, ARI.
SOMEDAY, IF HUMANS ARE EVEN REMEMBERED, THEY WILL BE KNOWN FOR WHAT THEY REALLY ARE...WEAK... AND STUPID--
EH?
STUPID PEOPLE, *SMART* GUNS.
CLICK
SMAK
SHOOMP
WHAT--?!
HRC
HELP ME!
I COMMAND YOU!

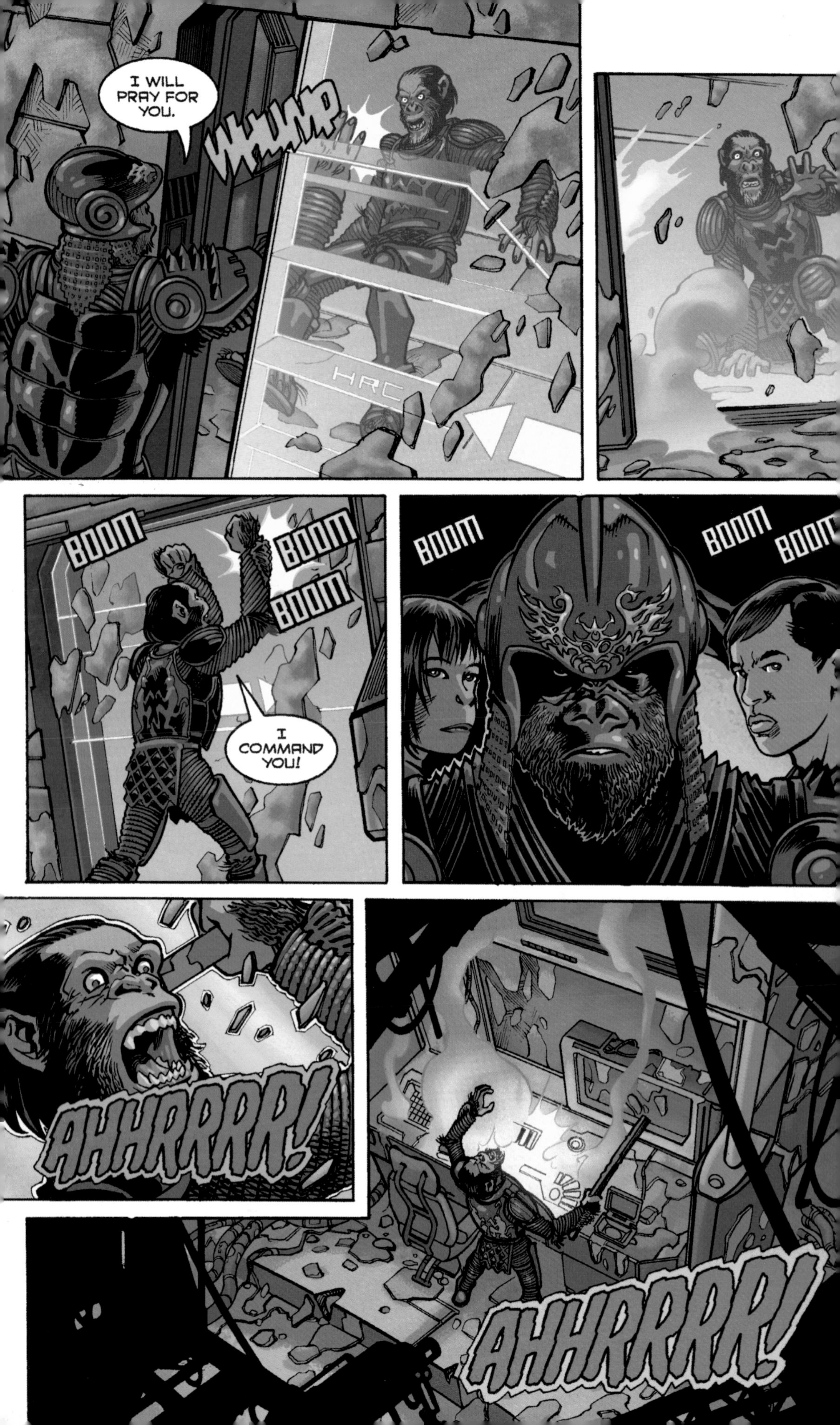
I WILL PRAY FOR YOU.
WHUMP
HRC
BOOM
BOOM
BOOM
I COMMAND YOU!
BOOM
BOOM
BOOM
AHHRRRR!
AHHRRRR!

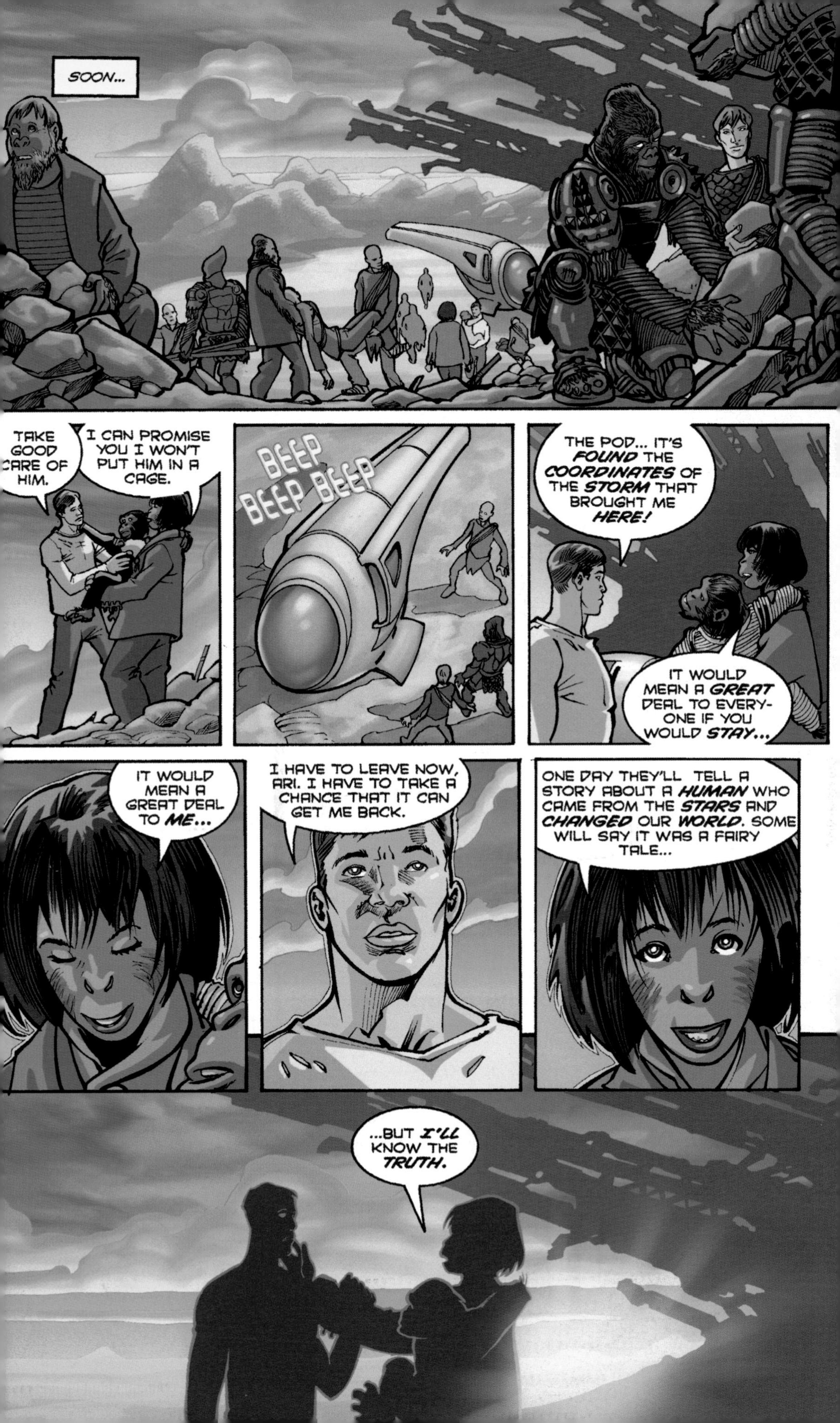
SOON...
TAKE GOOD CARE OF HIM.
I CAN PROMISE YOU I WON'T PUT HIM IN A CAGE.
BEEP BEEP BEEP
THE POD... IT'S FOUND THE COORDINATES OF THE STORM THAT BROUGHT ME HERE!
IT WOULD MEAN A GREAT DEAL TO EVERY-ONE IF YOU WOULD STAY...
IT WOULD MEAN A GREAT DEAL TO ME...
I HAVE TO LEAVE NOW, ARI. I HAVE TO TAKE A CHANCE THAT IT CAN GET ME BACK.
ONE DAY THEY'LL TELL A STORY ABOUT A HUMAN WHO CAME FROM THE STARS AND CHANGED OUR WORLD. SOME WILL SAY IT WAS A FAIRY TALE...
...BUT I'LL KNOW THE TRUTH.

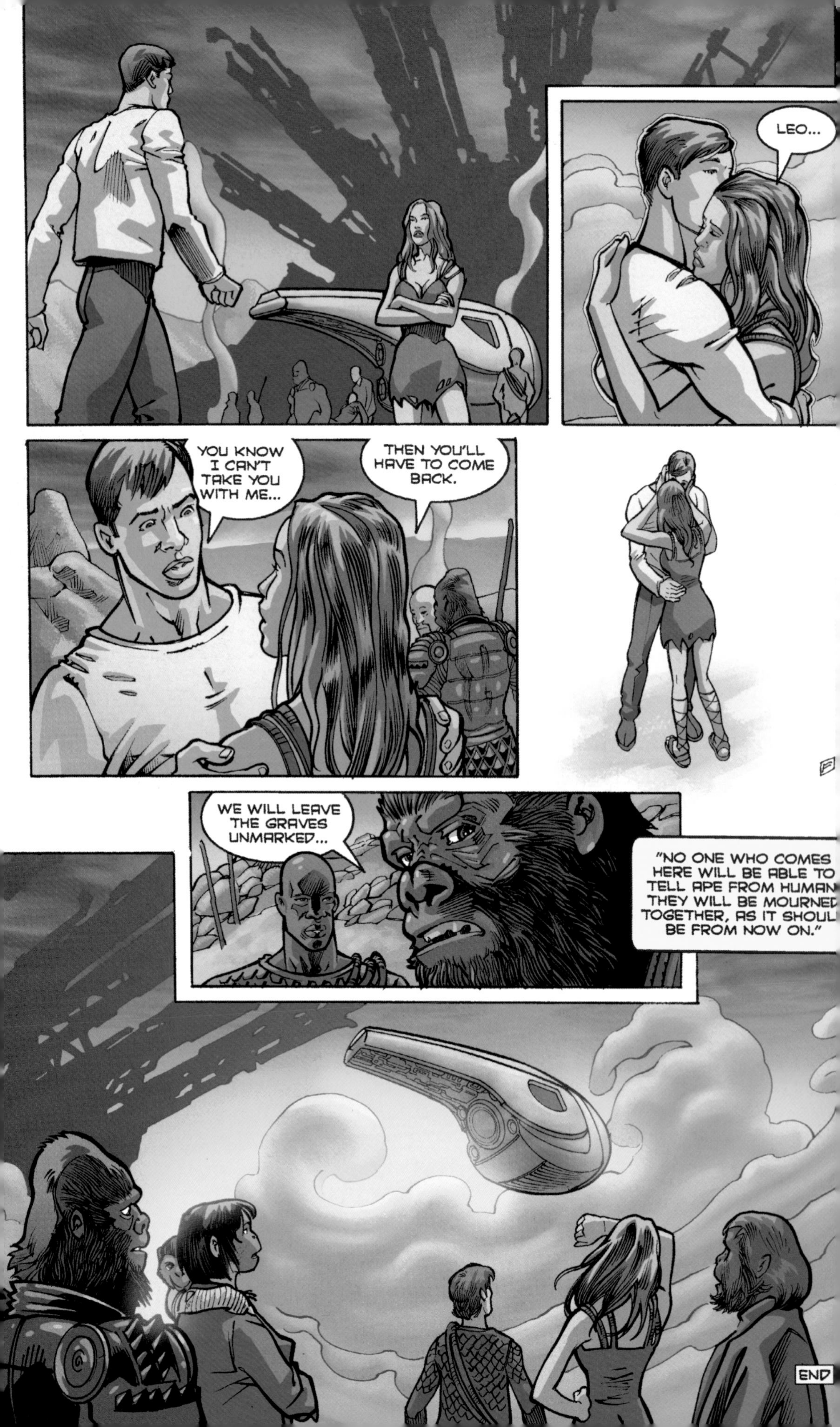
LEO...
YOU KNOW I CAN'T TAKE YOU WITH ME...
THEN YOU'LL HAVE TO COME BACK.
WE WILL LEAVE THE GRAVES UNMARKED...
"NO ONE WHO COMES HERE WILL BE ABLE TO TELL APE FROM HUMAN THEY WILL BE MOURNED TOGETHER, AS IT SHOUL BE FROM NOW ON."
END

PLANET OF THE APES ™

SKETCH GALLERY

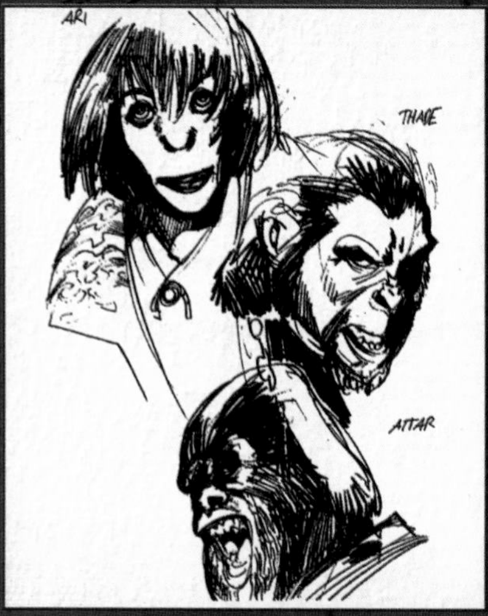
ARI
THADE
ATTAR

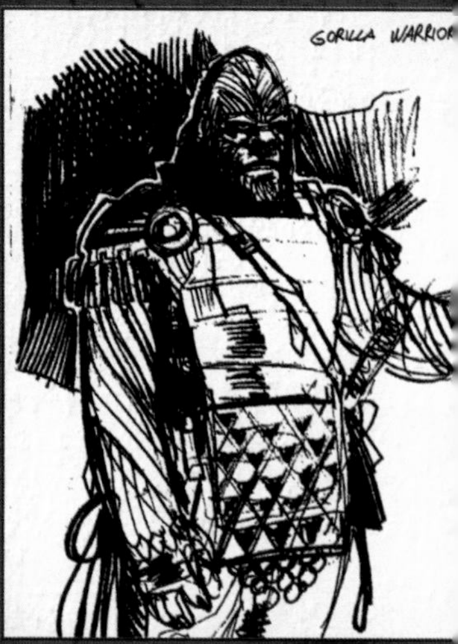
GORILLA WARRIOR

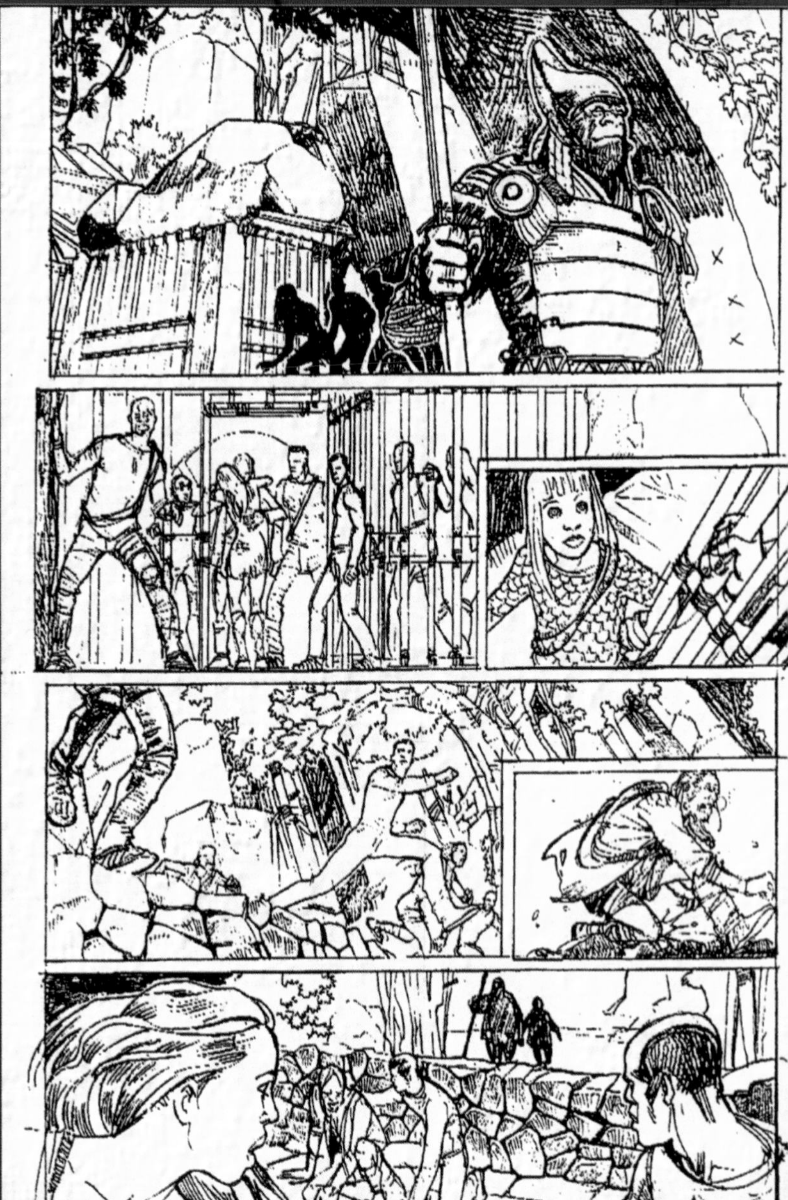

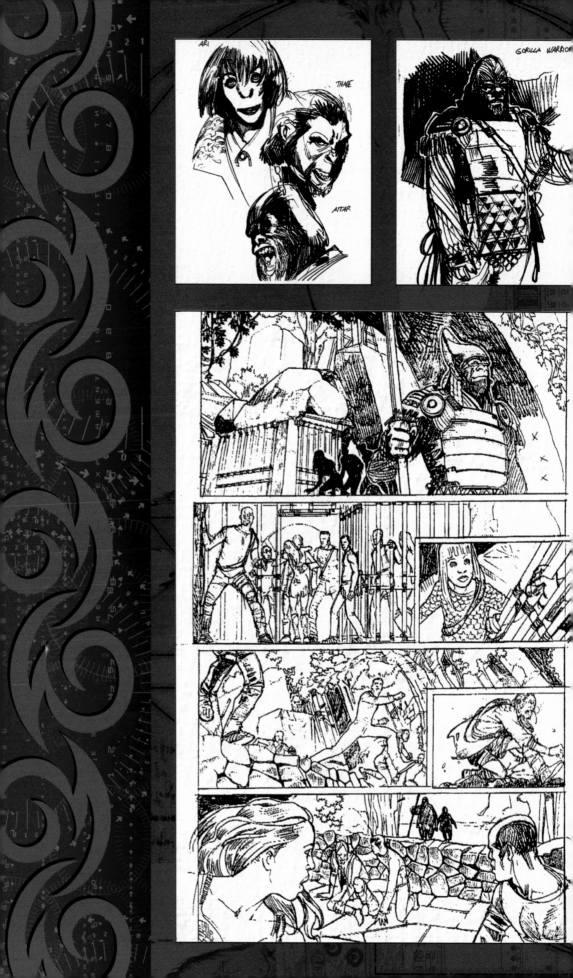

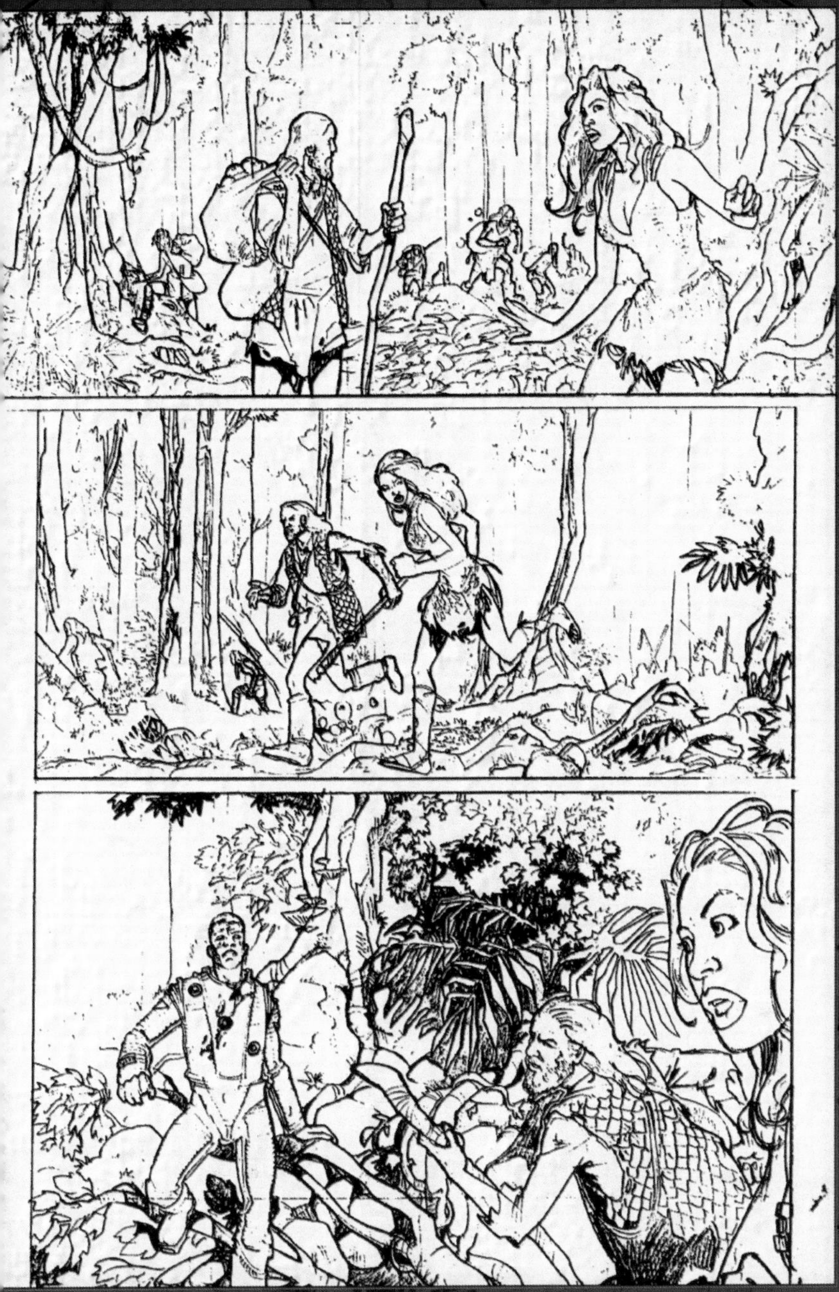

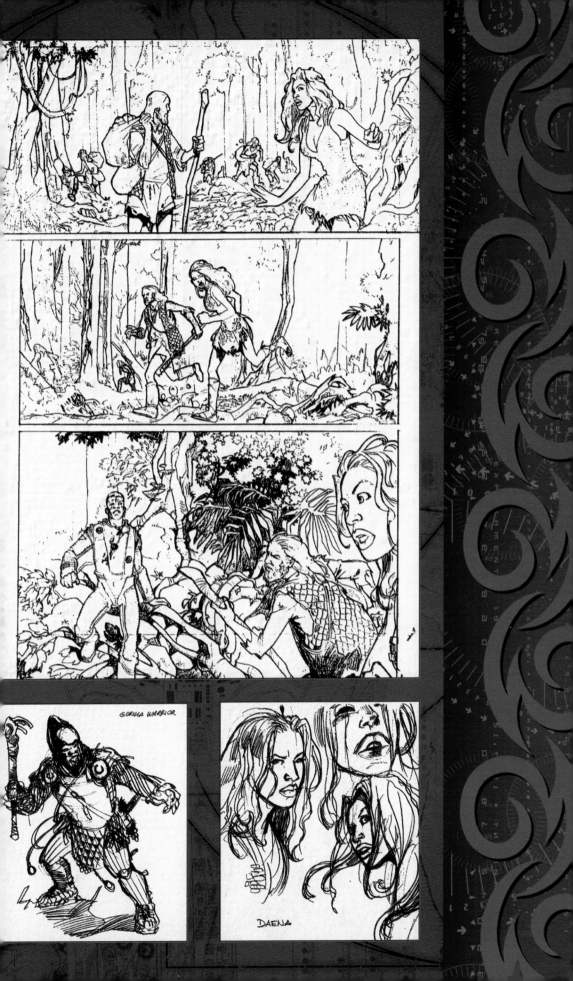

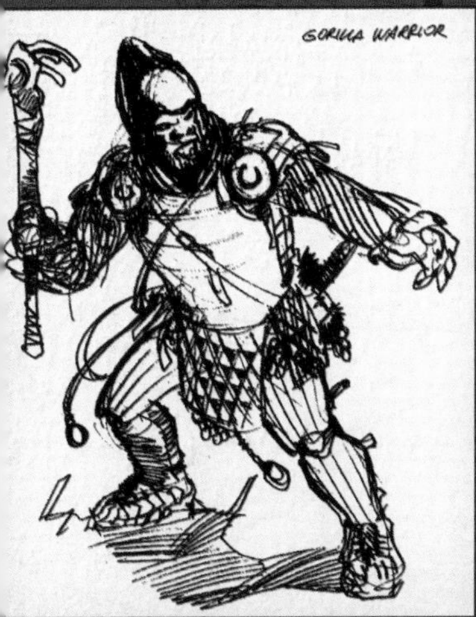
GORILLA WARRIOR

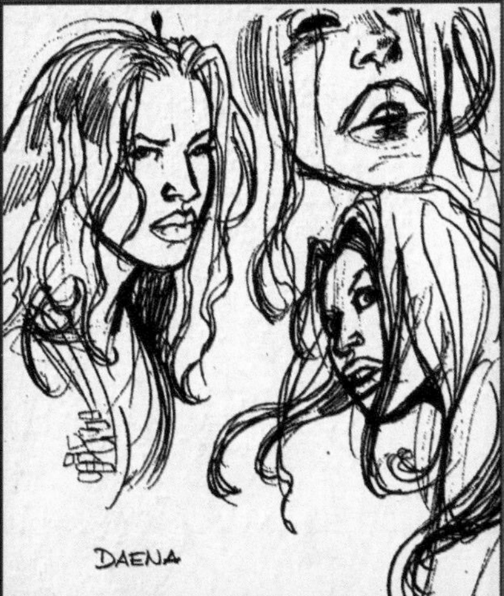
DAENA

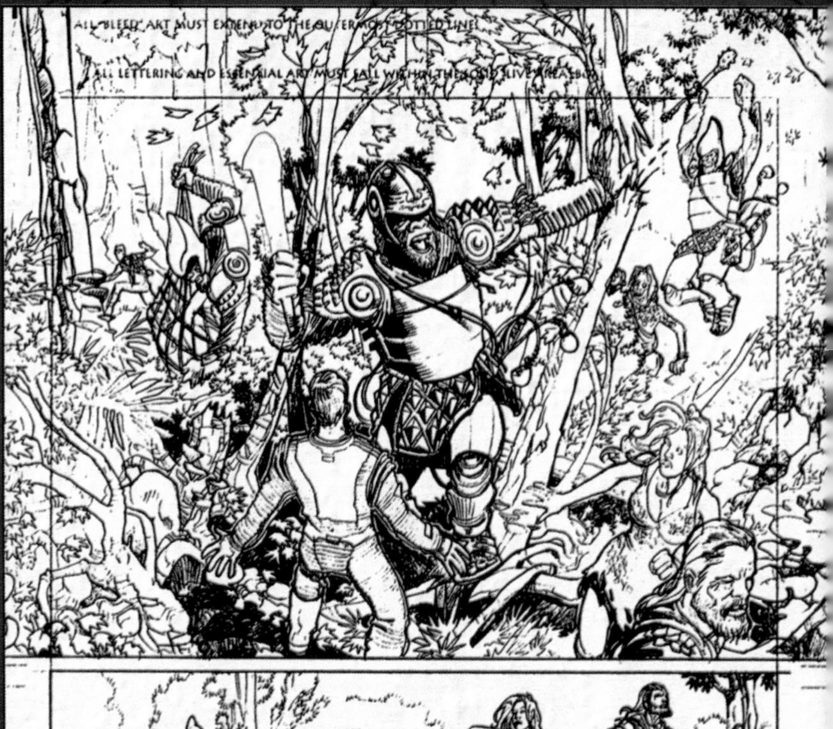

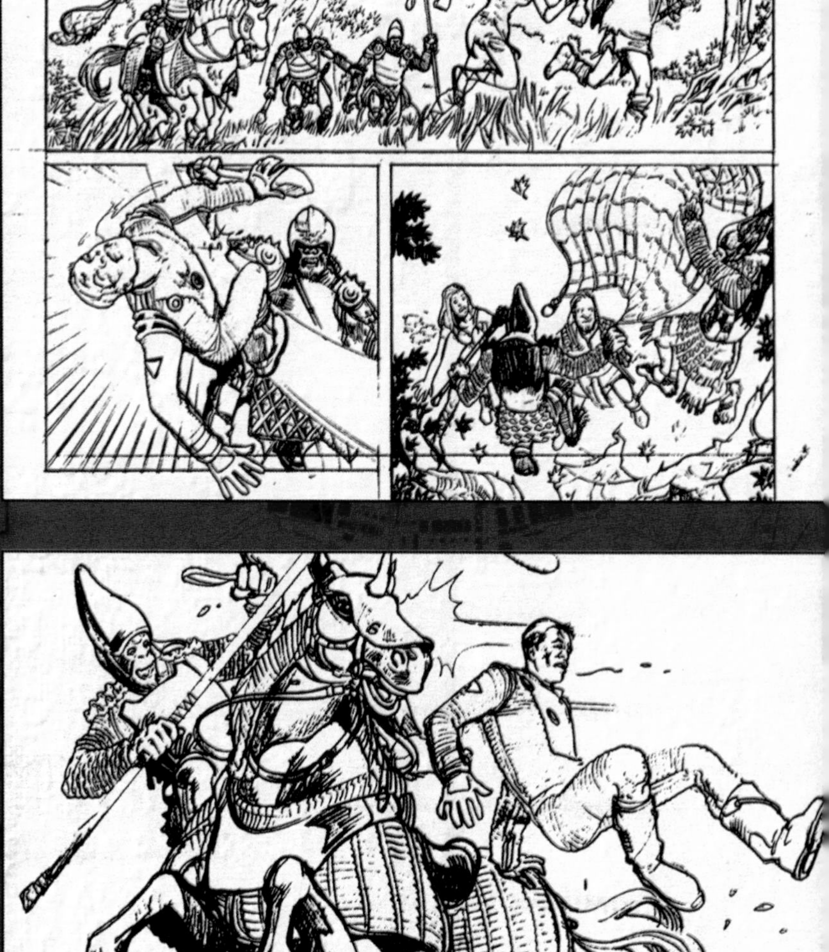

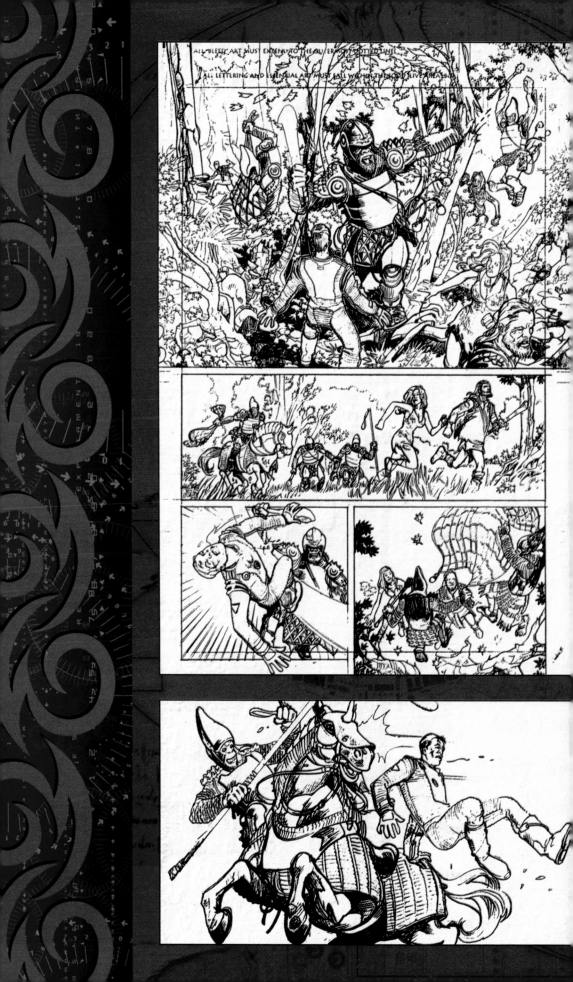

Look for these Buffy the Vampire Slayer trade paperbacks from Titan Books.

Buffy
the
Vampire Slayer
the Dust Waltz

The Dust Waltz
Brereton • Gomez • Florea
80-page color paperback
ISBN: 1-84023-057-6 **£7.99**

Buffy
the
Vampire Slayer
The Remaining Sunlight

The Remaining Sunlight
Watson • Bennett • Ketcham
80-page color trde paperback
ISBN: 1-84023-078-9 **£7.99**

Buffy
the
Vampire Slayer
the Origin

The Origin
Golden • Brereton • Bennett • Ketcham
80-page color paperback
ISBN: 1-84023-105-X **£7.99**

Buffy
the
Vampire Slayer
Uninvited Guests

Uninvited Guests
Watson • Gomez • Florea
104-page color paperback
ISBN: 1-84023-140-8 **£8.99**

Buffy
the
Vampire Slayer
Supernatural Defense Kit

Supernatural Defense Kit
Watson • Richards • Pimentel
30-page color hard cover
comes with golden-colored cross,
"claddagh" ring, and vial of "Holy water"
ISBN: 1-84023-165-3 **£19.99**

Buffy
the
Bad Blood

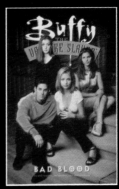

Bad Blood
Watson • Bennett • Ketcham
88-page color paperback
ISBN: 1-84023-179-3 **£8.99**

Buffy
the
Crash Test
Demons

Crash Test Demons
Watson • Richards • Pimentel
88-page color paperback
ISBN: 1-84023-199-8 **£8.99**

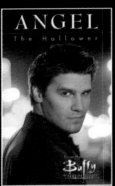

ANGEL
The Hollower
Buffy

Angel: The Hollower
Golden • Gomez • Florea
88-page color paperback
ISBN: 1-84023-163-7 **£8.99**

Buffy
the
Vampire Slayer
Ring of Fire

Coming Soon!
Ring of Fire
Petrie • Sook
80-page color paperback
ISBN: 1-84023-200-5

www.buffy.com

All publications are available through most good bookshops or dir from our mail order service at Titan Books. For a free graphic-no catalogue or to order, telephone 01858 433 169 with your credit-card de or contact Titan Books Mail Order, Bowden House, 36 Northampton Ro Market Harborough, Leics, LE16 9HE, quoting reference POTA/M

ART ASSISTANT
GORDON PURCELL
AND **DOMENICO NEZITI**

DESIGNER
DARIN FABRICK

ASSISTANT EDITOR
PHILIP SIMON

EDITOR
PHIL AMARA

PUBLISHER
MIKE RICHARDSON

PLANET OF THE APES
ISBN: 1 84023 379 6

Published by Titan Books, a division of Titan Publishing Group Ltd.
144 Southwark St
London SE1 0UP

A CIP catalogue record for this title is available from the British Library.

First edition July 2001
10 9 8 7 6 5 4 3 2 1

Printed in Italy.

What did you think of this book? We love to hear from our readers.
Please email us at: readerfeedback@titanemail.com or
write to us at the above address.

OTHER TITLES AVAILABLE FROM TITAN BOOKS

ALIENS

LABYRINTH
Woodring • Plunkett
136-page color paperback
ISBN: 1-85286-844-9

NIGHTMARE ASYLUM
(formerly Aliens: Book Two)
Verheiden • Beauvais
112-page color paperback
ISBN: 1-85286-765-5

OUTBREAK
(formerly Aliens: Book One)
Verheiden • Nelson
168-page color paperback
ISBN: 1-85286-756-6

ALIENS VS PREDATOR

ALIENS VS PREDATOR
Stradley • Norwood • Warner
176-page color paperback
ISBN: 1-85286-413-3

THE DEADLIEST OF THE SPECIES
Claremont • Guice • Barreto
320-page color paperback
ISBN: 1-85286-953-4

WAR
Various
200-page color paperback
ISBN: 1-85286-703-5

ETERNAL
Edginton • Maleev
88-page color paperback
ISBN: 1-84023-111-4

ALIENS VS. PREDATOR VS. TERMINTAOR
Schultz • Ruby • Ivy
96-page color paperback
ISBN: 1-84023-313-3

ANGEL

THE HOLLOWER
Golden • Gomez • Florea
88-page color paperback
ISBN: 1-84023-163-7

SURROGATES
Golden • Zanier •
Owens • Gomez
80-page color paperback
ISBN: 1-84023-234-X

BUFFY THE VAMPIRE SLAYER

THE DUST WALTZ
Brereton • Gomez
80-page color paperback
ISBN: 1-84023-057-6

THE REMAINING SUNLIGHT
Watson • Van Meter •
Bennett • Ross
88-page color paperback
ISBN: 1-84023-078-9

THE ORIGIN
Golden • Brereton •
Bennett • Ketcham
80-page color paperback
ISBN: 1-84023-105-X

RING OF FIRE
Petrie • Sook
80-page color paperback
ISBN: 1-84023-200-5

UNINVITED GUESTS
Watson • Brereton •
Gomez • Florea
96-page color paperback
ISBN: 1-84023-140-8

BAD BLOOD
Watson • Bennett • Ketcham
88-page color paperback
ISBN: 1-84023-179-3

CRASH TEST DEMONS
Watson • Richards • Pimentel
88-page color paperback
ISBN: 1-84023-199-8

PALE REFLECTIONS
Watson • Richards • Pimentel
96-page color paperback
ISBN: 1-84023-236-6

THE BLOOD OF CARTHAGE
Golden • Richards • Pimentel
128-page color paperback
ISBN: 1-84023-281-1

STAR WARS

BOBA FETT: ENEMY OF THE EMPIRE
Wagner • Gibson • Nadeau
112-page color paperback
ISBN: 1-84023-125-4

BOUNTY HUNTERS
Stradley • Truman • Schultz •
Mangels • Nadeau • Rubi • Saltares
112-page color paperback
ISBN: 1-84023-238-2

CHEWBACCA
Macan • Various
96-page color paperback
ISBN: 1-84023-274-9

CRIMSON EMPIRE
Richardson • Stradley •
Gulacy • Russell
160-page color paperback
ISBN: 1-84023-006-1

CRIMSON EMPIRE II
Richardson • Stradley •
Gulacy • Emberlin
160-page color paperback
ISBN: 1-84023-126-2

DARK EMPIRE
Veitch • Kennedy
184-page color paperback
ISBN: 1-84023-098-3

DARK EMPIRE II
Veitch • Kennedy
168-page color paperback
ISBN: 1-84023-099-1

EPISODE I THE PHANTOM MENACE
Gilroy • Damaggio • Williamson
112-page color paperback
ISBN: 1-84023-025-8

EPISODE I ADVENTURES
152-page color paperback
ISBN: 1-84023-177-7

JEDI ACADEMY – LEVIATHAN
Anderson • Carrasco • Heike
96-page color paperback
ISBN: 1-84023-138-6

THE LAST COMMAND
Baron • Biukovic • Shanower
144-page color paperback
ISBN: 1-84023-007-X

MARA JADE: BY THE EMPEROR'S HAND
Zahn • Stackpole • Ezquerra
144-page color paperback
ISBN: 1-84023-011-8

PRELUDE TO REBELLION
Strnad • Winn • Jones
144-page color paperback
ISBN: 1-84023-139-4

SHADOWS OF THE EMPIRE
Wagner • Plunkett • Russell
160-page color paperback
ISBN: 1-84023-009-6

SHADOWS OF THE EMPIRE: EVOLUTION
Perry • Randall • Simmons
120-page color paperback
ISBN: 1-84023-135-1

TALES OF THE JEDI: DARK LORDS OF THE SITH
Veitch • Anderson • Gossett
160-page color paperback
ISBN: 1-84023-129-7

TALES OF THE JEDI: FALL OF THE SITH
Anderson • Heike • Carrasco, Jr.
136-page color paperback
ISBN: 1-84023-012-6

TALES OF THE JEDI: THE GOLDEN AGE OF THE SITH
Anderson • Gossett •
Carrasco • Heike
144-page color paperback
ISBN: 1-84023-000-2

TALES OF THE JEDI: THE SITH WAR
152-page color paperback
ISBN: 1-84023-130-0

UNION
Stackpole • Teranishi • Chuckry
96-page color paperback
ISBN: 1-84023-233-1

VADER'S QUEST
Macan • Gibbons • McKie
96-page color paperback
ISBN: 1-84023-149-1

X-WING ROGUE SQUADRON: THE WARRIOR PRINCESS
Stackpole • Tolson •
Nadeau • Ensign
96-page color paperback
ISBN: 1-85286-997-6

X-WING ROGUE SQUADRON: REQUIEM FOR A ROGUE
Stackpole • Strnad • Erskine
112-page color paperback
ISBN: 1-84023-026-6

X-WING ROGUE SQUADRON: IN THE EMPIRE'S SERVICE
Stackpole • Nadeau • Ensign
96-page color paperback
ISBN: 1-84023-008-8

X-WING ROGUE SQUADRON: BLOOD AND HONOR
Stackpole • Crespo •
Hall • Johnson
96-page color paperback
ISBN: 1-84023-010-X

X-WING ROGUE SQUADRON: MASQUERADE
Stackpole • Johnson • Martin
96-page color paperback
ISBN: 1-84023-201-3

X-WING ROGUE SQUADRON: MANDATORY RETIREMENT
Stackpole • Crespo • Nadeau
96-page color paperback
ISBN: 1-84023-239-0

All publications are available through most good bookshops or direct from our mail-order service at Titan Books. For a free graphic-novels catalogue or to order, telephone 01858 433 169 with your credit-card details or contact Titan Books Mail Order, Bowden House, 36 Northampton Road, Market Harborough, Leics, LE16 9HE, quoting reference POTA/MA.